THE LAWS OF THE GAME OF RUGBY UNION

As framed by the
International Rugby Board

2000 edition

CONTENTS

	Page No:
FOREWORD	2
DEFINITIONS	4
BEFORE THE MATCH	9
1 The Ground	
2 The Ball	
3 Number of Players - The Team	
4 Players' Clothing	
5 Time	
6 Match Officials	
DURING THE MATCH	
Method of Playing the Match	32
7 Mode of Play	
8 Advantage	
9 Method of Scoring	
10 Foul Play	
11 Off-side and On-side in General Play	
12 Knock-on or Throw Forward	
In the Field-of-play	55
13 Kick-off and Restart Kicks	
14 Ball on the Ground - No Tackle	
15 Tackle : Ball-carrier Brought to the Ground	
16 Ruck	
17 Maul	
18 Mark	
Restarting the Game	78
19 Touch, Line-out and Line-out Off-side	
20 Scrum	
21 Penalty and Free Kicks	
In-Goal	111
22 In-goal	
UNDER 19 VARIATIONS	120
STANDARD SET OF VARIATIONS APPROPRIATE TO THE SEVEN-A-SIDE GAME	123
EXPERIMENTAL LAW VARIATIONS	129

FOREWORD

The Object of the Game is that two teams of fifteen, ten or seven players each, observing fair play according to the Laws and sporting spirit, should by carrying, passing, kicking and grounding the ball score as many points as possible, the team scoring the greater number of points being the winner of the match.

The Laws of the Game, including the Standard Set of Variations for Under 19 Rugby, are complete and contain all that is necessary to enable the game to be played correctly and fairly.

Rugby Union is a sport which involves physical contact. Any sport involving physical contact has inherent dangers. It is very important that players play the game in accordance with the Laws of the Game and be mindful of the safety of themselves and others. It is the responsibility of those who coach or teach the game to ensure that players are prepared in a manner which ensures compliance with the Laws of the Game and in accordance with safe practices.

It is the duty of the referee to apply fairly all the Laws of the Game in every match except when an experimental law has been authorised by the IRB Council.

It is the duty of the Unions to ensure that the Game at every level is conducted in accordance with disciplined and sporting behaviour. This principle cannot be upheld solely by the referee; its observance also rests on Unions, affiliated bodies and clubs.

ADMINISTRATION

1 **Proposals for changes in the Laws of the Game**

   Proposals together with any amendments to them, will be circulated to Unions and will be dealt with in accordance with Bye-Law 9.10.

2 **Submission of Proposals**

   Unions shall with each proposal set out:

   (a) the exact wording of the proposed alteration;
   (b) the object of the proposal; and
   (c the reason for it.

3 **Laws Committee**
   Pursuant to Bye-Law 9.13, the Council shall establish a standing Laws Committee consisting of not more than six representatives (to be appointed or re-appointed annually).

4 The functions of the Laws Committee

These are as follows:

(a) to consider and report on all proposals submitted by Unions to the Council for alterations in the Laws of the Game

(b) to recommend amendments to the wording of proposals and consequential alterations to give effect to its recommendations

(c) the Committee is not authorised to make recommendations which depart in principle, as distinct from detail, from specific proposals submitted by Unions; and

(d) to investigate and report on such matters as the Council may, from time to time, direct. Where appropriate, reports may include recommendations for alterations to the Laws of the Game for consideration by Unions.

5 Designated Members

The Laws Committee should each year appoint three of their members to be the Designated Members who will give interim rulings pursuant to the Council Minutes on that subject.

6 Rulings from Designated Members

(a) Rulings from the three Designated Members should only be sought in cases in which the Union concerned was itself unable to give a Ruling after full consideration of the point by their appropriate Committee. Only cases of real doubt or difficulty related to incidents in actual play, and not to hypothetical cases, should be referred to the Council. In all such references for a Ruling the Unions should state its own opinion as to what the correct ruling ought to be, as this will be helpful to the three Designated Members.

(b) All decisions of the three Designated Members on applications for Rulings are to be submitted to the Council for consideration as alterations to the Laws.

(c) The Chairman of the Laws Committee shall indicate which Rulings are to be submitted to the Council for consideration as alterations to the Laws.

DEFINITIONS

Advantage - Law 8 - Advantage
Attacking Team - the team who are in their opponents half when the play is taking place there.
Ball-carrier - a player carrying the ball
Beyond or Behind or In Front of a Position - with both feet, except where the context makes that inappropriate
Binding - grasping firmly another player's body from the shoulder to the hips with the whole arm from hand to shoulder
Cavalry Charge - Law 10 - Foul Play
Conversion Kick - Law 9 - Method of Scoring
Converted - a conversion kick that was successful
Dangerous Play - Law 10 - Foul play
Dead - the ball is out of play. This happens when the ball has gone outside the playing area and remained there, or when the referee has blown the whistle to indicate a stoppage, or when a conversion kick has been taken
Dead Ball Line - Law 1 - The Ground
Defending Team - the team in whose half of the ground play is taking place; their opponents are the Attacking Team
Drop Kick - the ball is dropped from the hand or hands to the ground and kicked as it rises from its first bounce
Drop Out - Law 13 - Kick-off and Restart kicks
Dropped Goal - Law 9 - Method of Scoring
Field-of-Play - Law 1 - The Ground
Flanker - forward player who usually wears jersey No.6 or No.7
Flying Wedge - Law 10 - Foul Play
Foul Play - Law 10 - Foul Play
Free Kick - a kick awarded to the non-offending team for an infringement by their opponents; unless a law states otherwise, a free kick awarded because of an infringement is awarded at the place of infringement
Front Row Players - forward players who are made up of loose-head prop, hooker and tight-head prop
Goal-line - Law 1 - The Ground
Grounding the Ball - Law 22 - In-goal
Half Time - the interval between the two halves of the game
Hindmost Foot - the foot of the hindmost player in a scrum, ruck or maul which is nearest that player's goal-line
Hooker - the middle front row player in a scrum
In-field - away from touch and towards the middle of the field
In-goal - Law 22 - In-goal
Kick - a kick is made by hitting the ball with any part of the leg or foot, except the heel, from the toe to the knee but not including the knee; a kick must move the ball a visible distance out of the hand, or along the ground
Kick-off - Law 13 - Kick-off and Restart Kicks

Knock-on - Law 12 - Knock-on or Throw-forward
Lifting - Law 19 - Touch, Line-out and Line-out Off-side
Line-of-touch - an imaginary line at right angles to the touch-line at the place where the ball is thrown in from touch
Line-out - Law 19 - Touch, Line-out and Line-out Off-side
Line Through the Mark or Place - unless stated otherwise, a line parallel to the touch-line
Long Throw - Law 19 - Touch, Line-out and Line-out Off-side
Loose-head Prop - the left front row player in a scrum
Match Organiser - the organisation responsible for the match which may be a union, a group of unions or an organisation affiliated to the International Rugby Board
Mark - Law 18 - Mark
Maul - Law 15 - Maul
No side - the end of the match.
Obstruction - Law 10 - Foul Play
Off-side in Open Play - Law 11 - Off-side and On-side in general play
Off-side Line - an imaginary line across the ground, from one touch-line to the other, parallel to the goal-lines; the position of this line varies according to the Law
Off-side the 10 Metre Law - Law 11 - Off-side and On-side in General Play
On-side - Law 11 - Off-side and On-side in General Play
Open or Bleeding Wound - Law 3 - Number of Players - The Team
Out of Play - this happens when the ball or the ball carrier has gone into touch or touch-in-goal, or touched or crossed the dead-ball line
Oversteps - a player steps across a line with one or both feet; the line may be real (for example, goal-line) or imaginary (for example, off-side line)
Pass - a player throws the ball to another player; if a player hands the ball to another player without throwing it, this is also a pass
Peeling Off - Law 19 - Touch, Line-out and Line-out Off-side
Penalty Goal - Law 9 - Method of Scoring
Penalty Kick - a kick awarded to the non-offending team for an infringement by their opponents; unless a Law says otherwise, a penalty kick is awarded at the place of infringement
Penalty Try - Law 10 - Foul Play
Place Kick - the ball is kicked after it has been placed on the ground for that purpose
Placer - a player who holds the ball on the ground for a team-mate to kick
Played - the ball is played when it is touched by a player
Playing Area - Law 1 - The Ground
Playing Enclosure - Law 1 - The Ground
Possession - this happens when a player is carrying the ball or a team has the ball in its control; for example, the ball in one half of a scrum or ruck is in that team's possession
Prop - a front row player
Punt - the ball is dropped from the hand or hands and kicked before it touches the ground
Pushover Try - Law 22 - In-goal

Receiver - Law 19 - Touch, Line-out and Line-out Off-side
Repeated Infringements - Law 10 - Foul Play
Replacements - Law 3 - Number of players - The Team
Ruck - Law 16 - Ruck
Scrum - formerly named 'scrummage'; this happens when players from each team come together in scrum formation so that play can be started by throwing the ball into the scrum
Scrum Half - a player nominated to throw the ball into a scrum
Substitutes - Law 3 - Number of Players - The Team
Tackle - Law 15 - Tackle: Ball-carrier Brought to the Ground
Team-mate - another player of the same team
The 22 - Law 1 - The Ground
Throw-forward - Law 12 - Knock-on or Throw-forward
Throw-in - the act of the player who throws in to scrum or line-out
Tight-head Prop - the right front row player in a scrum
Touch - Law 19 - Touch, Line-out and Line-out Off-side
Touch Down - Law 22 - In-goal
Touch-line - Law 1 - The Ground
Touch-In-Goal Line - Law 1 - The Ground
Touch Judge - Law 6 - Match Officials
Try - Law 9 - Method of Scoring
Union - the controlling body under whose jurisdiction the match is played; for an international match it means the International Rugby Board or a Committee of the Board

Rugby Union is a sport which involves physical contact. Any sport involving physical contact has inherent dangers. It is very important that players play the game in accordance with the Laws of the Game and be mindful of the safety of themselves and others. It is the responsibility of those who coach or teach the game to ensure that players are prepared in a manner which ensures compliance with the Laws of the Game and in accordance with safe practices.

iRB
INTERNATIONAL RUGBY BOARD

BEFORE THE MATCH

Law 1 The Ground
Law 2 The Ball
Law 3 Number of Players - The Team
Law 4 Players' Clothing
Law 5 Time
Law 6 Match Officials

BEFORE THE MATCH

The following six Laws of the Game cover all the necessary requirements before the match can proceed.

These laws outline the need for a ground with specific measurements and a ball of specified size, weight and air pressure.

These laws recognise the need for two teams and indicate what they can wear to play the game of rugby.

These laws also indicate the time constraints placed on a rugby match and outline the role of the match officials.

LAW 1 - THE GROUND

DEFINITIONS

The Ground is the total area shown on the plan. The Ground includes:

The Field-of-play is the area (as shown on the plan) between the goal-lines and the touch-lines. These lines are not part of the field-of-play.

The Playing Area is the field-of-play and the in-goal areas (as shown on the plan). The touch-lines, touch-in-goal lines and dead-ball lines are not part of the playing area.

The Playing Enclosure is the playing area and a space around it, not less than 5 metres where practicable, which is known as the **perimeter area**.

In-goal is the area between the goal-line and the dead-ball line, and between the touch-in-goal lines. It includes the goal-line but it does not include the dead-ball line or the touch-in-goal lines.

'The 22' is the area between the goal-line and the 22-metre line, including the 22-metre line but excluding the goal-line.

The Plan, including all the words and figures on it, is part of the laws.

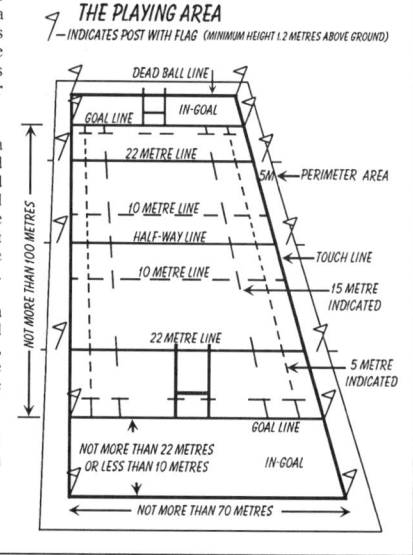

THE PLAYING AREA
— INDICATES POST WITH FLAG (MINIMUM HEIGHT 1.2 METRES ABOVE GROUND)

- DEAD BALL LINE
- GOAL LINE
- IN-GOAL
- 22 METRE LINE
- 10 METRE LINE
- HALF-WAY LINE
- 10 METRE LINE
- 22 METRE LINE
- GOAL LINE
- IN-GOAL
- PERIMETER AREA
- TOUCH LINE
- 15 METRE INDICATED
- 5 METRE INDICATED
- NOT MORE THAN 100 METRES
- NOT MORE THAN 22 METRES OR LESS THAN 10 METRES
- NOT MORE THAN 70 METRES

LAW 1 - THE GROUND

1   SURFACE OF THE PLAYING ENCLOSURE

Surface. The surface is grass, but if this is not possible it may be clay or sand, provided it is not dangerous. Any permanently hard surface, for example asphalt or cement, is prohibited.

2   REQUIRED DIMENSIONS FOR THE PLAYING ENCLOSURE

(a)   **Dimensions.** The field-of-play does not exceed 100 metres in length and 70 metres in width. Each in-goal does not exceed 22 metres in length and 70 metres in width.

(b)   The length and breadth of the playing area are as near as possible to the dimensions indicated. All the areas are rectangular.

(c)   The distance from the goal-line to the dead-ball line is not less than 10 metres where practicable.

3   LINES ON THE PLAYING ENCLOSURE

(a)   **Solid lines**

The dead ball lines and touch-in-goal lines, both of which are outside the in-goal areas;

The goal-lines, which are within the In-goal areas but outside the field-of-play;

The 22-metre lines; which are parallel to the goal-lines

The half-way line which is parallel to the goal-lines; and

The touch-lines which are outside the field-of-play.

(b)   **Broken Lines**

The 10-metre lines, which run from one touch-line to the other, and 10 metres from each side of the half-way line and parallel to it; and

The 5-metre lines, which run from one goal-line to the other, parallel to the touch-lines.

LAW 1 - THE GROUND

(c) **Dash Lines**

Six lines, each 1 metre long, 5 metres in from each of the goal-lines, positioned 5 metres and 15 metres from each touch-line and one in front of each goal post.

Seven dash lines, each 1 metre long, 15 metres in from each of the touch-lines, intersecting the goal-lines, the 22-metre lines, the 10-metre lines and the half-way line and ending at the goal-lines.

One dash line of half a metre long intersects the centre of the half-way line.

All the lines must be suitably marked out according to the plan.

4 DIMENSIONS FOR GOAL POSTS AND CROSS BARS

(a) The distance between the two goal posts is 5.6 metres.

(b) The crossbar is placed between the two goal posts so that its top edge is 3.0 metres from the ground.

(c) The minimum height of the goal posts is 3.4 metres.

(d) When padding is attached to the goal-posts the distance from the goal-line to the external edge of the padding must not exceed 300mm.

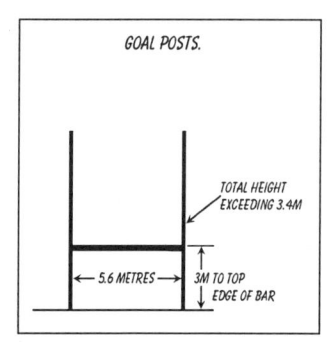

GOAL POSTS.

TOTAL HEIGHT EXCEEDING 3.4M

← 5.6 METRES → *3M TO TOP EDGE OF BAR*

LAW 1 - THE GROUND

5 FLAG POSTS

(a) There are 14 flag posts with flags, each with a minimum height of 1.2 metres above the ground.

(b) Flag posts must be positioned at the intersection of touch-in-goal lines and the goal-lines and at the intersection of the touch-in-goal lines and the dead ball lines. These eight flag posts are outside the in-goal area and do not form part of the playing area.

(c) Flag posts must be positioned in line with the 22-metre lines and the half-way line, 2 metres outside the touch-lines and within the playing enclosure.

6 OBJECTIONS TO THE GROUND

(a) If either team has objections about the ground or the way it is marked out they must tell the referee before the match starts.

(b) The referee will attempt to resolve the issues but must not start a match if any part of the ground is considered to be dangerous.

LAW 2 - THE BALL

1 SHAPE

The ball must be oval and made of four panels.

2 DIMENSIONS

Length in line	280 - 300 millimetres
Circumference (end to end)	760 - 790 millimetres
Circumference (in width)	580 - 620 millimetres

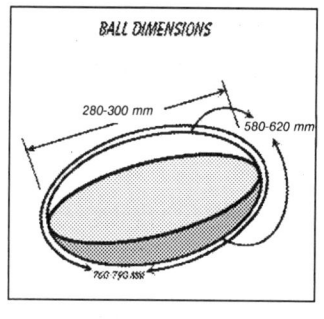

BALL DIMENSIONS

280-300 mm
580-620 mm
760-790 mm

3 MATERIALS

Leather or similar synthetic material. It may be treated to make it resistant to mud and easier to grip.

4 WEIGHT

400 - 440 grams

5 AIR PRESSURE AT THE START OF PLAY

0.67 - 0.70 kilograms per square centimetre, or $9^1/_2$ -10 lbs per square inch.

6 SPARE BALLS

Spare balls may be available during a match, but a team must not gain or attempt to gain an unfair advantage by using them or changing them.

7 SMALLER BALLS

The dimensions and weight of the ball may be reduced for matches between young players.

LAW 3 - NUMBER OF PLAYERS - THE TEAM

DEFINITIONS

A Team. A team consists of fifteen players who start the match plus any authorised replacements and/or substitutes.

Replacement. A player who replaces an injured team mate.

Substitute. A player who replaces a team mate for tactical reasons.

1 MAXIMUM NUMBER OF PLAYERS ON THE PLAYING AREA

Maximum: each team must have no more than fifteen players on the playing area.

2 TEAM WITH MORE THAN THE PERMITTED NUMBER OF PLAYERS

Objection: at any time before or during a match a team may make an objection to the referee about the number of players in their opponents' team. As soon as the referee knows that a team has too many players, the referee must order the captain of that team to reduce the number appropriately. The score at the time of the objection remains unaltered.

3 WHEN THERE ARE FEWER THAN FIFTEEN PLAYERS

A Union may authorise matches to be played with fewer than fifteen players in each team. When that happens, all the Laws of the Game apply except that each team must have at least five players in the scrum at all times.

Exception: matches between teams of seven-a-side are an exception. These matches are covered by the Seven-a-Side Variations to the Laws of the Game.

4 PLAYERS NOMINATED AS SUBSTITUTES

For international matches a Union may nominate up to seven replacements/substitutes. For other matches, the Union with jurisdiction over the match decides how many replacements/substitutes may be nominated.

LAW 3 - NUMBER OF PLAYERS - THE TEAM

5 SUITABLY TRAINED AND EXPERIENCED PLAYERS IN THE FRONT ROW

(a) The table below indicates the numbers of suitably trained and experienced players for the front row when nominating different numbers of players.

No. of Players	Number of Suitably Trained and Experienced Players
15 or less	3 players who can play in the front row
16, 17 or 18	4 players who can play in the front row
19, 20, 21 or 22	5 players who can play in the front row

(b) Each player in the front row and the potential replacement must be suitably trained and experienced.

The replacement of a front row forward may come from suitably trained and experienced players who started the match or from the nominated replacements.

6 SENT OFF FOR FOUL PLAY

A player sent off for foul play must not be replaced or substituted. For an exception to this Law, refer to Law 3 14 Page 19.

7 PERMANENT REPLACEMENT

A player may be replaced if injured. If the player is permanently replaced, that player must not return and play in that match. The replacement of the injured player must be made when the ball is dead and with the permission of the referee.

8 THE DECISION FOR PERMANENT REPLACEMENT

(a) When a national representative team is playing in a match, a player may be replaced only when, in the opinion of a doctor, the player is so injured that it would be unwise for that player to continue playing in that match.

LAW 3 - NUMBER OF PLAYERS - THE TEAM

(b) In other matches, where a Union has given explicit permission, an injured player may be replaced on the advice of a medically trained person. If none is present, that player may be replaced if the referee agrees.

9 THE REFEREE'S POWER TO STOP AN INJURED PLAYER FROM CONTINUING

If the referee decides – with or without the advice of a doctor or other medically qualified person – that a player is so injured that the player should stop playing, the referee may order that player to leave the playing area. The referee may also order an injured player to leave the field in order to be medically examined.

10 TEMPORARY REPLACEMENT

(a) When a player leaves the field to have bleeding controlled and/or an open wound covered, that player may be temporarily replaced. There is no time limit on that player's absence from the match.

(b) If the replacement is injured, that player may also be replaced.

(c) If the replacement is sent off for foul play, the replaced player may not return to the field-of-play.

11 PLAYER WISHING TO REJOIN THE MATCH

(a) A player who has an open or bleeding wound must leave the playing area. The player must not return until the bleeding is controlled and the wound has been covered.

(b) A player who leaves a match because of injury or any other reason must not rejoin the match until the referee permits the player to return. The referee must not let a player rejoin a match until the ball is dead.

(c) If the player rejoins the match without the referee's permission, and the referee believes the player did so to help that player's team or obstruct the opposing team, the referee penalises the player for misconduct.

(d) If the referee believes that this offence was not voluntary interference but the offending player's team gained an advantage from the return, the referee orders a scrum where the player rejoined the match, and the opposing team throws in the ball.

LAW 3 - NUMBER OF PLAYERS - THE TEAM

12 NUMBER OF SUBSTITUTIONS

A team can substitute up to two front row players and up to five other players. Substitutions may only be made when the ball is dead and with the permission of the referee.

13 SUBSTITUTED PLAYERS REJOINING THE MATCH

If a player is substituted, that player must not return and play in that match even to replace an injured player.

Exception 1: a substituted player may replace a player with a bleeding or open wound.

Exception 2: a substituted player may replace a front row player when injured, temporarily suspended or sent off.

14 FRONT ROW FORWARD SENT OFF OR TEMPORARILY SUSPENDED

(a) If a front row player is sent off or temporarily suspended the referee will ask that player's captain whether or not the team has another player on the field of play who is suitably trained to play in the front row. If not, the captain chooses any player from that team. That player leaves the field-of-play and is replaced by a suitably trained front-row player from the team's replacements. The captain may do this either immediately or after another player has been tried in the front row.

(b) Furthermore, if, because of sending-off or injury, a team cannot provide enough suitably trained front-row players, the match continues with uncontested scrums (14 (c)).

(c) An uncontested scrum is the same as a normal scrum, except that the teams do not compete for the ball, the team throwing in the ball must win it, and neither team is allowed to push, and:

In a full scrum, the formation must be 3-4-1 (i.e., 3-4-1 in the front, second and third rows respectively).

If a team is one player short, then both teams must be in a 3-4 formation (i.e. with no No.8).

If a team is two players short, then both teams must be in a 3-2-1 formation (i.e. no flankers).

If a team is three players short, then both teams must be in a 3-2 formation (i.e. only front rows and locks).

LAW 4 – PLAYERS' CLOTHING

DEFINITION

Players' clothing is anything players wear.

A player wears a jersey, shorts and underwear, socks and boots.

1 ADDITIONAL ITEMS OF CLOTHING

(a) A player may wear supports made of elasticated or compressible materials which must be washable.

(b) A player may wear shin guards worn under the socks with padding incorporated in non-rigid fabric with no part of the padding thicker than 0.5 cm when compressed.

(c) A player may wear ankle supports worn under socks, not extending higher than one third of the length of the shin and, if rigid, from material other than metal.

(d) A player may wear mitts (fingerless gloves).

(e) A player may wear shoulder pads, made of soft and thin materials, which may be incorporated in an undergarment or jersey provided that the pads cover the shoulder and collar bone only. No part of the pads may be thicker than 1cm when uncompressed. No part of the pads may have a density of more than 45 kilograms per cubic metre.

(f) A player may wear a mouth guard or dental protector.

(g) A player may wear headgear made of soft and thin materials provided that no part of the headgear is thicker than 1 cm when uncompressed and no part of the headgear has a density of more than 45 kilograms per cubic metre.

(h) A player may wear bandages and/or dressings to cover or protect any injury.

(i) A player may wear thin tape or other similar material as support and/or to prevent injury.

LAW 4 - PLAYERS CLOTHING

2 SPECIAL ADDITIONAL ITEMS FOR WOMEN

Besides the previous items, women may wear chest pads made of soft and thin materials which may be incorporated as part of a garment provided that the pads cover the shoulder and/or collar bone and/or chest only with no part of the pads thicker than 1 cm when uncompressed and no part of the pads having a density of more than 45 kilograms per cubic metre.

3 THICKNESS AND DENSITY

The measurement of thickness and density includes any other material incorporated in the pads or used to secure the pads to the body.

4 STUDS

(a) Studs of players' boots must conform to British Standard BS6366 1983 or an equivalent standard.

(b) Studs of players' boots must be circular; and securely fastened to the sole of the boot.

(c) Studs of players' boots must have the following dimensions:
Not longer than 18 mm, measured from the sole; a minimum diameter of 10 mm at the top of the stud; a minimum diameter of 13 mm at the base of the stud (excluding the washer); and a minimum diameter of 20 mm at the base where the stud integrates with the washer.

(d) Moulded rubber multi-studded soles are acceptable provided they have no sharp edges or ridges.

CORRECT SIZE OF STUDS

The maximum and minimum dimensions of a stud are shown here. Alternatively, a player may wear boots with moulded rubber multi-studded soles.

5 BANNED ITEMS OF CLOTHING

(a) A player must not wear any item that is contaminated by blood.

(b) A player must not wear any item that is sharp or abrasive.

(c) A player must not wear any items containing buckles, clips, rings, hinges, zippers, screws, bolts or rigid material or projection not otherwise permitted under this law.

LAW 4 - PLAYERS CLOTHING

(d) A player must not wear jewellery such as rings or earrings.

(e) A player must not wear gloves.

(f) A player must not wear shorts with padding sewn into them.

(g) A player must not wear any item of which any part is thicker than 0.5 cm when uncompressed or is denser than 45 kilograms per cubic metre unless specified within this law.

(h) A player must not wear any item that is normally permitted by law, but, in the referee's opinion that is liable to cause injury to a player.

(i) A player must not wear a single stud at the toe of the boot.

6 AUTHORISED MARK FOR PADDED ITEMS

From 1 October 2000, shoulder pads, headgear and chest pads must bear the authorised mark of the IRB to indicate that they conform to this law.

7 INSPECTION OF PLAYERS' CLOTHING

(a) The referee or the touch judges appointed by or under the authority of the match organiser inspect the players' clothing and studs for conformity to this law.

(b) The referee has power to decide at any time, before or during the match, that part of a player's clothing is dangerous or illegal. If the referee decides that clothing is dangerous or illegal the referee must order the player to remove it. The player must not take part in the match until the items of clothing are removed.

(c) If, at an inspection before the match, the referee or a touch judge tells a player that an item banned under this law is being worn, and the player is subsequently found to be wearing that item on the field-of-play, that player is sent off for misconduct.

Penalty: A penalty kick is awarded at the place where play is restarted.

8 WEARING OTHER CLOTHING

Any player requiring or wishing to wear any dressing, protection, padding, support or such like material other than that specified within this law is not permitted to play in a match.

The referee must not allow any player to leave the playing area to change items of clothing, unless these are bloodstained.

LAW 5 - TIME

1 DURATION OF A MATCH

A match lasts no longer than eighty minutes plus time lost, extra time and any special conditions. A match is divided into two halves each of not more than forty minutes playing time.

2 HALF TIME

After half time the teams change ends. There is an interval of not more than 10 minutes. The length of the interval is decided by the match organiser, the Union or the recognised body which has jurisdiction over the game. During the interval the teams, the referee and the touch judges may leave the playing enclosure.

3 TIME KEEPING

The referee keeps the time but may delegate the duty to either or both the touch judges in which case the referee signals to them any stoppage of time or time lost. If the referee is in doubt as to the correct time the referee consults either or both of the touch judges and may consult others but only if the touch judges cannot help.

4 TIME LOST

Time lost may be due to the following:

(a) **Injury.** The referee may stop play for not more than one minute so that an injured player can be treated, or for any other permitted delay.

The referee may allow play to continue while a medically trained person treats an injured player in the playing area or the player may go to the touch-line for treatment.

If the referee believes that the player is feigning injury, the referee arranges for the player to be removed from the playing area, and re-starts play at once. Alternatively, the referee may allow play to continue while a medically trained person examines the player in the playing area.

(b) **Replacing players' clothing.** When the ball is dead, the referee allows time for a player to replace or repair a badly torn jersey, shorts or boots. Time is allowed for a player to re-tie a boot-lace.

LAW 5 - TIME

(c) **Replacement and substitution of players.** Time is allowed when a player is replaced or substituted.

(d) **Reporting of foul play by a touch judge.** Time is allowed when a touch judge reports foul play.

5 MAKING UP FOR TIME LOST

Any playing time lost is made up in the same half of the match.

6 PLAYING EXTRA TIME

A match may last more than eighty minutes if the Union has authorised the playing of extra time in a drawn match in a knock-out competition.

7 OTHER TIME REGULATIONS

(a) In international matches, play always lasts eighty minutes plus lost time.

(b) In non-international matches a Union may decide the length of a match.

(c) If the Union does not decide, the teams agree on the length of a match. If they cannot agree, the referee decides.

(d) The referee has power to declare no side at any time, if the referee believes that play should not go on because it would be dangerous.

(e) If time expires and the ball is not dead or an awarded scrum, line-out, mark, free kick or penalty kick has not been completed, the referee allows play to continue until the next time when the ball becomes dead, unless a penalty kick or free kick has been awarded.

(f) If time expires after a try has been scored the referee allows time for the conversion kick to be taken.

LAW 6 - MATCH OFFICIALS

LAW 6 - MATCH OFFICIALS

DEFINITIONS

Every match is under the control of Match Officials who consist of the Referee and two Touch Judges. Additional persons as authorised by the match organisers may include the referee and/or touch judge reserve, an official to assist the referee in making decisions by using technological devices, the time keeper, the Match Doctor, the team doctors, the non-playing members of the teams and the ball persons.

A. REFEREE

BEFORE THE MATCH

1 APPOINTING THE REFEREE

The referee is appointed by the match organiser. If no referee has been appointed the two teams may agree upon a referee. If they cannot agree, the home team appoints a referee.

2 REPLACING THE REFEREE

If the referee is unable to complete the match, the referee's replacement is appointed according to the instructions of the match organiser. If the match organiser has given no instructions, the referee appoints the replacement. If the referee cannot do so, the home team appoints a replacement.

3 DUTIES OF THE REFEREE BEFORE THE MATCH

(a) **Toss.** The referee organises the toss. One of the captains tosses a coin and the other captain calls to see who wins the toss. The winner of the toss decides whether to kick-off or to choose an end. If the winner of the toss decides to choose an end, the opponents must kick-off and vice versa.

(b) **Players' clothing inspection.** The referee must inspect the players' clothing to ensure it is in compliance with Law 4. The referee may delegate responsibility for the inspection of players' clothing to the touch judges.

(c) **Touch judges.** The referee may instruct the touch judges as to their duties.

4 LIMITATION ON THE REFEREE

The referee must not give advice to either team before the match.

LAW 6 - MATCH OFFICIALS

DURING THE MATCH

5 THE DUTIES OF THE REFEREE IN THE PLAYING ENCLOSURE

(a) The referee is the sole judge of fact and of law during a match. The referee must apply fairly all the Laws of the Game in every match.

(b) When the match organiser has authorised the application of an experimental law as approved by the IRB Council, the referee may apply these laws in prescribed matches.

(c) The referee keeps the time.

(d) The referee keeps the score.

(e) The referee gives permission to the players to leave the playing area.

(f) The referee gives permission to the replacements or substitutes to enter the playing area.

(g) The referee gives permission to the team doctors or medically trained persons or their assistants to enter the playing area, as and when permitted by the Law.

(h) The referee gives permission to each of the coaches to enter the playing area at half time to attend their teams during the interval.

6 PLAYERS DISPUTING A REFEREE'S DECISION

All players must respect the authority of the referee. They must not dispute the referee's decisions. They must stop playing at once when the referee blows the whistle except at a kick-off.

7 REFEREE ALTERING A DECISION

The referee may alter a decision when a touch judge has raised the flag to signal touch or an act of foul play.

8 REFEREE CONSULTING WITH OTHERS

(a) The referee may consult with touch judges in regard to matters relating to their duties, the law relating to foul play, or time keeping.

LAW 6 - MATCH OFFICIALS

(b) A match organiser may appoint an official who uses technological devices. If the referee is unsure when making a decision in in-goal involving a try being scored or a touch down, that official may be consulted.

(c) The official may be consulted in relation to the success or otherwise of kicks at goal.

(d) The official may be consulted if the referee or touch judge is unsure if a player was or was not in-touch when attempting to ground the ball to score a try.

(e) The official may be consulted if the referee or touch judges are unsure when making decisions relating to touch-in-goal and the ball being made dead if a score may have occurred.

(f) A match organiser may appoint a time keeper who will signify the end of each half.

(g) The referee must not consult with any other persons.

9 THE REFEREE'S WHISTLE

(a) The referee must carry a whistle and blow the whistle to indicate the beginning and end of each half of the match.

(b) The referee has power to stop play at any time.

(c) The referee must blow the whistle to indicate a score, or a touch-down.

(d) The referee must blow the whistle to stop play because of an infringement or for an offence of foul play. When the referee cautions or sends off the offender, the referee must whistle a second time when the penalty kick or penalty try is awarded.

(e) The referee must blow the whistle when the ball has gone out of play, or when it has become unplayable, or when a penalty is awarded.

(f) The referee must blow the whistle when the ball or the ball-carrier touches the referee and either team gains an advantage from this.

(g) The referee must blow the whistle when it would be dangerous to let play continue. This includes when a scrum collapses, or when a front-row player is lifted into the air or is forced upwards out of a scrum, or when it is probable that a player has been seriously injured.

LAW 6 - MATCH OFFICIALS

(h) The referee may blow the whistle to stop play for any other reason according to the laws.

10 YELLOW AND RED CARDS

(a) When a player has been cautioned the referee will show that player a yellow card.

(b) When a player has been sent off, the referee will show that player a red card

11 THE REFEREE AND INJURY

(a) If a player is injured and continuation of play would be dangerous, the referee must blow the whistle immediately.

(b) If the referee stops play because a player has been injured, and there has been no infringement and the ball has not been made dead, play restarts with a scrum. The team last in possession throws in the ball. If neither team was in possession, the attacking team throws in the ball.

(c) The referee must blow the whistle if continuation of play would be dangerous for any reason.

12 THE BALL TOUCHING THE REFEREE

(a) If the ball or the ball-carrier touches the referee and neither team gains an advantage, play continues.

(b) If either team gains an advantage in the field-of-play, the referee orders a scrum and the team that last played the ball has the throw-in.

(c) If either team gains an advantage in in-goal, if the ball is in possession of an attacking player the referee awards a try where the contact took place.

(d) If either team gains an advantage in in-goal, if the ball is in possession of a defending player, the referee awards a touch-down where the contact took place.

13 THE BALL IN IN-GOAL TOUCHED BY NON-PLAYER

The referee judges what would have happened next and awards a try or a touchdown at the place where the ball was touched.

LAW 6 - MATCH OFFICIALS

AFTER THE MATCH

14 SCORE

The referee communicates the score to the teams and to the match organiser.

15 PLAYER SENT-OFF

If a player is sent off the referee gives the match organiser a written report on the foul play infringement as soon as possible.

B. TOUCH JUDGES

BEFORE THE MATCH

1 APPOINTING TOUCH JUDGES

There are two touch judges for every match. Unless they have been appointed by or under the authority of the match organiser, each team provides a touch judge.

2 REPLACING A TOUCH JUDGE

The match organiser may nominate a person to act as a replacement for the referee or the touch judges. This person is called the reserve touch judge and stands in the perimeter area.

3 CONTROL OF TOUCH JUDGES

The referee has control over both touch judges. The referee may tell them what their duties are, and may overrule their decisions. If a touch judge is unsatisfactory the referee may ask that the touch judge be replaced. If the referee believes a touch judge is guilty of misconduct, the referee has power to send the touch judge off and make a report to the match organiser.

LAW 6 - MATCH OFFICIALS

DURING THE MATCH

4 WHERE THE TOUCH JUDGES SHOULD BE

(a) There is one touch judge on each side of the ground. The touch judge remains in touch except when judging a kick at goal. When judging a kick at goal the touch judges stand in in-goal behind the goal posts.

(b) A touch judge may enter the playing area when reporting an offence of dangerous play or misconduct to the referee. The touch judge may do this only at the next stoppage in play.

5 TOUCH JUDGE SIGNALS

(a) Each touch judge carries a flag or something similar with which to signal decisions.

(b) **Signalling result of kick at goal.** When a conversion kick or a penalty kick at goal is being taken, the touch judges must help the referee by signalling the result of the kick. One touch judge stands at or behind each goal post. If the ball goes over the cross-bar and between the posts, the touch judge raises the flag to indicate a goal.

(c) **Signalling touch.** When the ball or the ball-carrier has gone into touch, the touch judge must hold up the flag. The touch judge must stand at the place of throw-in and point to the team entitled to throw in. The touch judge must also signal when the ball or the ball carrier has gone into touch-in-goal.

LAW 6 - MATCH OFFICIALS

(d) **When to keep the flag raised.** When the ball is thrown in, the touch judge must lower the flag, with the following exceptions:

Exception 1: When the player throwing in puts any part of either foot in the field-of-play, the touch judge keeps the flag up.

Exception 2: When the team not entitled to throw-in has done so, the touch judge keeps the flag up.

Exception 3: When, at a quick throw-in, the ball that went into touch is replaced by another ball, or after it went into or it has been touched by anyone except the player who takes the throw-in, the touch judge keeps the flag up.

(e) It is for the referee, and not the touch judge, to decide whether or not the ball was thrown in from the correct place.

(f) Signalling dangerous play. A touch judge signals that dangerous play or misconduct has been seen by holding the flag horizontally and pointing infield at right angles to the touch-line.

LAW 6 - MATCH OFFICIALS

6 AFTER SIGNALLING FOUL PLAY

A match organiser may give authority to the touch judge to signal for foul play. If a touch judge signals foul play, the touch judge must stay in touch and continue to carry out all the other duties until the next stoppage in play. The touch judge may then enter the playing area to report the offence to the referee. The referee may then take whatever action is needed. Any penalty awarded will be in accordance with the law of foul play (Law 10).

AFTER THE MATCH

7 PLAYER SENT-OFF

If a player has been sent-off following a touch judge's signal, the touch judge submits a written report about the incident to the referee as soon as possible after the match and provides it to the match organiser.

C. ADDITIONAL PERSONS

1 RESERVE TOUCH JUDGE

When a reserve touch judge is appointed, the referee's authority regarding replacements and substitutions may be delegated to the reserve touch judge.

2 THOSE WHO MAY ENTER THE PLAYING AREA

The match doctor and the non-playing members of the team may enter the playing area as authorised by the referee.

3 LIMITS TO ENTERING THE PLAYING AREA

In the case of injury, these persons may enter the playing area while play continues, provided they have permission from the referee. Otherwise, they enter only when the ball is dead.

iRB
INTERNATIONAL RUGBY BOARD

DURING THE MATCH

Method of Playing the Match

Law 7		Mode of Play
Law 8		Advantage
Law 9		Method of Scoring
Law 10		Foul Play
Law 11		Off-side/On-side in General Play
Law 12		Knock-on or Throw Forward

HOW THE GAME IS PLAYED

All the necessary requirements for the game to commence have been covered. The following five laws indicate how the game is played. The Laws cover the mode of play (Law 7), how continuity of the game is maintained through the application of advantage (Law 8), how a team scores (Law 9), the requirement of players to remain on-side (Law 11), the need for players to play within the Laws of the Game and not to commit acts of foul play (Law 10). While playing the game it is possible that they may knock the ball on or throw it forward in contravention of the law (Law 12).

LAW 7 - MODE OF PLAY

PLAYING A MATCH

A match is started by a kick-off.

After the kick-off, any player who is on-side may take the ball and run with it.

Any player may throw it or kick it.

Any player may give the ball to another player.

Any player may tackle, hold or shove an opponent holding the ball.

Any player may fall on the ball.

Any player may take part in a scrum, ruck, maul or line-out.

Any player may ground the ball in an in-goal.

Whatever a player does must be in accordance with the Laws of the Game.

LAW 8 - ADVANTAGE

DEFINITION

The law of advantage takes precedence over most other laws and its purpose is to make play more continuous with fewer stoppages for infringements. Players are encouraged to play to the whistle despite infringements by their opponents. When the result of an infringement by one team is that their opposing team may gain an advantage, the referee does not whistle immediately for the infringement.

1 ADVANTAGE IN PRACTICE

(a) The referee is sole judge of whether or not a team has gained an advantage. The referee has wide discretion when making decisions.

(b) Advantage can be either territorial or tactical.

(c) Territorial advantage means a gain in ground.

(d) Tactical advantage means freedom for the non-offending team to play the ball as they wish.

2 WHEN ADVANTAGE DOES NOT ARISE

The advantage must be clear and real. A mere opportunity to gain advantage is not enough. If the non-offending team does not gain an advantage, the referee blows the whistle and brings play back to the place of infringement.

LAW 8 - ADVANTAGE

3 WHEN THE ADVANTAGE LAW IS NOT APPLIED

(a) **Referee contact.** Advantage must not be applied when the ball, or a player carrying it, touches the referee.

(b) **Ball out of tunnel.** Advantage must not be applied when the ball comes out of either end of the tunnel at a scrum without having been played.

(c) **Wheeled scrum.** Advantage must not be applied when the scrum is wheeled through more than 90 degrees (so that the middle line has passed beyond a position parallel to the touch-line).

(d) **Collapsed scrum.** Advantage must not be applied when a scrum collapses. The referee must blow the whistle immediately.

(e) **Player lifted in the air.** Advantage must not be applied when a player in a scrum is lifted in the air or forced upwards out of the scrum. The referee must blow the whistle immediately.

4 IMMEDIATE WHISTLE WHEN NO ADVANTAGE

The referee blows the whistle immediately once the referee decides an advantage cannot be gained by the non-offending team.

5 MORE THAN ONE INFRINGEMENT

(a) If there is more than one infringement by the same team the referee applies the advantage law.

(b) If advantage is being played following an infringement by one team and then the other team commit an infringement, the referee blows the whistle and applies the sanctions associated with the first infringement.

LAW 9 - METHOD OF SCORING

LAW 9 – METHOD OF SCORING

A. SCORING POINTS   Value

1   POINTS VALUES

Try. When an attacking player is first to ground the ball in the
opponents' in-goal, a try is scored.   5 points

Penalty Try. If a player would probably have scored a try but for
foul play by an opponent, a penalty try is awarded between the
goal posts.   5 points

Conversion Goal. When a player scores a try it gives the
player's team the right to attempt to score a goal by taking a kick
at goal; this also applies to a penalty try. This kick is a
conversion kick: a conversion kick can be a place kick or a
drop kick.   2 points

Penalty Goal. A player scores a penalty goal by kicking a goal
from a penalty kick.   3 points

Dropped Goal. A player scores a dropped goal by kicking a goal
from a drop kick in general play. The team awarded a free kick
cannot score a dropped goal until after the ball next becomes dead,
or after an opponent has played or touched it, or has tackled the
ball-carrier or a maul has been formed. This restriction applies
also to a scrum taken instead of a free kick.   3 points

Goal. A player scores a goal by kicking the ball over an
opponents' cross bar and between the goal posts from the
field-of-play, by a place kick or drop kick.
A goal cannot be scored from a kick-off, a drop-out or a free kick.

2   KICK AT GOAL - SPECIAL CIRCUMSTANCES

(a) If, after the ball is kicked, it touches the ground or any team-mate of the kicker,
     a goal cannot be scored.

(b) If the ball has crossed the cross bar a goal is scored, even if the wind blows it
     back into the field-of-play.

LAW 9 - METHOD OF SCORING

(c) If an opponent commits an offence as the kick at goal is being taken, but nevertheless the kick is successful, advantage is played and the score stands.

(d) If an opponent illegally touches the ball as the kick at goal is being taken and the kick is not successful, the referee may award a goal if the referee considers that one would otherwise probably have been scored.

B CONVERSION KICK

DEFINITION

When a player scores a try, it gives the player's team the right to try to score a goal by taking a kick at goal; this also applies to a penalty try. This kick is a conversion kick. A conversion kick can be a place kick or a drop kick.

1 TAKING A CONVERSION KICK

(a) The kicker must use the ball that was in play unless it is defective.

(b) The kick is taken on a line through the place where the try was scored.

(c) A placer is a team-mate who holds the ball for the kicker to kick.

(d) The kicker may place the ball directly on the ground or on sand, sawdust or a kicking tee approved by the Union.

(e) The kicker must take the kick within one minute from the time the kicker has indicated an intention to kick.

Penalty: The kick is disallowed if the kicker does not take the kick within the time allowed.

(f) The scoring team may choose not to take a conversion kick.

LAW 9 - METHOD OF SCORING

2 THE KICKER'S TEAM

(a) All the kicker's team, except the placer, must be behind the ball when it is kicked.

(b) Neither the kicker nor a placer must do anything to mislead their opponents into charging too soon.

(c) If the ball falls over before the kicker begins the approach to kick, the referee permits the kicker to replace it without excessive delay. While the ball is replaced, the opponents must stay behind their goal-line.

If the ball falls over after the kicker begins the approach to kick, the kicker may then kick or attempt a dropped goal.

If the ball falls over and rolls away from the line through the place where the try was scored, and the kicker then kicks the ball over the cross bar, a goal is scored.

If the ball falls over and rolls into touch after the kicker begins the approach to kick, the kick is disallowed.

Penalty: (a)-(c) If the kicker's team infringes, the kick is disallowed.

3 THE OPPOSING TEAM

(a) All the opposing team must be behind their goal-line until the kicker begins the approach to kick or starts to kick. When the kicker does this, they may charge or jump so as to try to prevent a goal.

(b) When the ball falls over after the kicker began the approach to kick, the opponents may continue to charge.

(c) A defending team must not shout during a kick at goal.

Penalty: (a)-(c) If the opposing team infringes but the kick is successful, the goal stands.

If the kick is unsuccessful, the kicker may take another kick and the opposing team is not allowed to charge.

When another kick is allowed, the kicker may repeat all the preparations. The kicker may change the type of kick.

LAW 10 – FOUL PLAY

DEFINITION

Foul play is anything a person does within the playing enclosure that is against the letter and spirit of the Laws of the Game. It includes obstruction, unfair play, repeated infringements, dangerous play and misconduct.

1 OBSTRUCTION

(a) **Charging or pushing.** When a player and an opponent are running for the ball, either player must not charge or push the other except shoulder-to-shoulder.

   Penalty: Penalty Kick (PK)

(b) **Running in front of a ball-carrier.** A player must not voluntarily move or stand in front of a team-mate carrying the ball.

   Penalty: Penalty Kick (PK)

(c) **Blocking the tackler.** A player must not voluntarily move or stand in a position that prevents an opponent from tackling a ball-carrier.

   Penalty: Penalty Kick (PK)

(d) **Blocking the ball.** A player must not voluntarily move or stand in a position that prevents an opponent from playing the ball.

   Penalty: Penalty Kick (PK)

LAW 10 - FOUL PLAY

(e) **Ball-carrier running into team-mate at a set-piece.**
A player carrying the ball after it has left a scrum, ruck, maul or line-out must not run into team-mates in front of the player.

Penalty: Penalty Kick (PK)

(f) **Flanker obstructing opposing scrum-half.**
A flanker in a scrum must not prevent an opposing scrum-half from advancing around the scrum.

Penalty: Penalty Kick (PK)

(g) A player carrying the ball cannot be penalised for obstruction under any circumstances.

2 UNFAIR PLAY

(a) **Intentionally offending.** A player must not voluntarily infringe any Law of the Game, or play unfairly

Penalty: Penalty Kick (PK)

A penalty try must be awarded if the offence prevents a try that would probably otherwise have been scored.

(b) **Time-wasting.** A player must not voluntarily waste time.

Penalty: Free Kick (FK)

(c) **Throwing into touch etc.** A player must not voluntarily knock-on or throw the ball into touch, touch-in-goal, or over the dead-ball line.

Penalty: Penalty Kick (PK)

A penalty try must be awarded if the offence prevents a try that would probably otherwise have been scored.

For an offence in the player's In-goal, the mark for the kick is 5 metres from the goal-line in line with the place of infringement.

LAW 10 - FOUL PLAY

3 REPEATED INFRINGEMENTS

(a) **Repeatedly offending.** A player must not repeatedly infringe any law. Repeated infringement is a matter of fact. The question of whether or not the player intended to infringe is irrelevant.

Penalty: Penalty Kick (PK)

If necessary, the player is cautioned. If the player repeats the offence, the player must be sent off.

(b) **Infringements.** The problem of repeated infringements usually arises with the scrum, line-out, off-side, ruck, maul or tackle laws. A player penalised for several infringements of one of these laws is cautioned. If the player repeats the offence, the player is sent off.

(c) **Repeated infringements by the team.** When different players of the same team repeatedly commit the same offence, the referee must decide whether or not this amounts to repeated infringement. If it does, the referee gives a general warning to the team and if they then repeat the offence the referee sends off the guilty player(s).

Penalty: Penalty Kick (PK)

A penalty try must be awarded if the offence prevents a try that would probably otherwise have been scored.

(d) **Repeated infringements: standard applied by referee.** When the referee decides how many offences constitute repeated infringement, the referee must always apply a strict standard in representative and senior matches. When a player offends three times the referee must caution that player.

The referee may relax this standard in junior or minor matches, where infringements may be the result of ignorance of the laws or lack of skill.

4 DANGEROUS PLAY AND MISCONDUCT

(a) **Punching or striking.** A player must not strikes an opponent with the fist or arm, including the elbow, shoulder, head or knee(s).

Penalty: Penalty Kick (PK)

LAW 10 - FOUL PLAY

(b) **Stamping or trampling.** A player must not stamp or trample on an opponent.

   Penalty: Penalty Kick (PK)

(c) **Kicking.** A player must not kick an opponent

   Penalty: Penalty Kick (PK)

(d) **Tripping.** A player must not trip an opponent with the leg or foot.

   Penalty: Penalty Kick (PK)

(e) **Dangerous tackling.** A player must not tackle an opponent early, late (PK) or dangerously.

   A player must not tackle (or try to tackle) an opponent (PK) above the line of the shoulders. A tackle around the opponent's neck or head is dangerous play.

   A "stiff-arm tackle" is (PK) dangerous play. A player makes a stiff-arm tackle when using a stiff arm to strike an opponent.

   Playing a player without the (PK) ball is dangerous play.

   DANGEROUS PLAY: HIGH TACKLE

   The referee decides whether or not a tackle is dangerous. The referee takes into account the circumstances, such as the apparent intentions of the tackler, or the nature of the tackle, or the defenceless position of the player being tackled or knocked over. Any of these may result in serious injury.

   All forms of dangerous tackling must be punished severely. A player who commits this type of foul must be sent off. Advantage may be played, but if the offence prevents a probable try, a penalty try must be awarded.

   In open play, a player must not tackle an opponent whose feet are off the ground because that player is jumping to catch the ball.

   Penalty: Penalty Kick (PK)

LAW 10 - FOUL PLAY

(f) **Playing an opponent without the ball.** Except in a scrum, ruck or maul, a player must not hold, or push, or charge into, or obstruct an opponent not carrying the ball.

Penalty: Penalty Kick (PK)

(g) **Dangerous charging.** A player must not charge or knocks down an opponent carrying the ball without trying to grasp that player.

Penalty: Penalty Kick (PK)

(h) **Tackling the jumper in the air.** A player must not tap or pull the foot or feet of an opponent jumping for the ball in a line-out.

Penalty: Penalty Kick (PK)

DANGEROUS PLAY: TACKLING THE JUMPER IN THE AIR

(i) **Dangerous play in a scrum, ruck or maul.** The front row of a scrum must not rush against its opponents.

Front-row players must not voluntarily lift opponents off their feet or force them upwards out of the scrum.

Players must not voluntarily collapse a scrum, ruck or maul.

Players must not charge into a ruck or maul without binding onto a team-mate.

Penalty: Penalty Kick (PK)

(j) **Retaliation.** A player must not retaliate. Even if an opponent is infringing the laws, a player must not do anything that is dangerous to the opponent.

Penalty: Penalty Kick (PK)

(k) **Acts contrary to good sportsmanship.** A player must not do anything that is against the spirit of good sportsmanship in the playing enclosure.

Penalty: Penalty Kick (PK)

LAW 10 - FOUL PLAY

The player who commits an act of dangerous play or misconduct must either be sent off or else be cautioned that a send-off will result if the offences are repeated or a similar offence committed. After a caution, if the player commits the same or a similar offence, the player must be sent off. A penalty try must be awarded if the offence prevents a try that would probably otherwise have been scored.

(l) **Misconduct while the ball is out of play.** A player, must not, while the ball is out of play, commit any misconduct, or obstruct or in any way interfere with an opponent.

Penalty: Penalty Kick

The penalty is the same as for sections 10.4 (a)-(k) except that the penalty kick is awarded at the place where play would restart. If that place is on the touch-line or within 15 metres of it, the mark for the penalty kick is on the 15-metre line, in line with that place.

If play would restart at a 5-metre scrum, the mark for the penalty kick is at that place at least 15 metres from the touch-line.

If play would restart with a drop-out, the non-offending team may choose to take the penalty kick anywhere on the 22-metre line.

If a penalty kick is awarded but the offending team is guilty of further misconduct before the kick is taken, the referee cautions or orders off the guilty player and advances the mark for the penalty kick 10 metres. This covers both the original offence and the misconduct.

If a penalty kick is awarded to a team but a player of that team is guilty of further misconduct before the kick is taken, the referee cautions or orders off the guilty player, declares the kick disallowed, and awards a penalty kick to the opposing team.

If an offence is committed outside the playing area while the ball is still in play, and if that offence is not covered by any other part of this law, the penalty kick is awarded on the 15-metre line, in line with where the offence happened.

For an offence reported by a touch judge a penalty kick may be awarded where the offence happened, or advantage may be played.

LAW 10 - FOUL PLAY

(m) **Late-charging the kicker.** A player must not voluntarily charge or obstruct an opponent who has just kicked the ball.

Penalty: The non-offending team may choose to take the penalty kick either at the place of infringement or where the ball lands.

Place of infringement. If the infringement happens in the kicker's in-goal, the mark for the penalty kick is 5 metres from the goal-line in line with the actual place of infringement.

If the infringement happens in touch, the mark for the penalty kick is on the 15-metre line in line with the place of the actual infringement.

If the infringement happens in touch-in-goal, the mark for the penalty kick is 5 metres from the goal-line and 15 metres from the touch-line.

Where the ball lands. If the ball lands in touch, the mark for the optional penalty kick is on the 15-metre line in line with where it went into touch. If the ball lands within 15 metres of the touch-line, the mark is on the 15-metre line opposite where it landed.

If the ball lands in the in-goal, in touch-in-goal, or on or over the dead-ball line, the mark for the optional penalty kick is 5 metres from the goal-line, in line with the place where the ball crossed the goal-line and at least 15 metres from the touch-line.

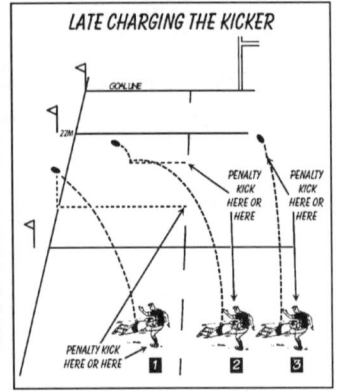

If the ball hits a goal post or cross bar, the optional penalty kick is awarded where the ball lands on the ground.

46

LAW 10 - FOUL PLAY

(n) **Flying Wedge and Cavalry Charge.** A team must not use the "Flying Wedge" or the "Cavalry Charge".

Penalty: Penalty Kick at the place of the original infringement. (PK)

'Flying Wedge' The type of attack known as a 'Flying Wedge' usually happens near the goal-line, when the attacking team is awarded a penalty kick or free kick.

The kicker tap-kicks the ball and starts the attack, either by driving towards the goal-line or by passing to a team-mate who drives forward. Immediately, team-mates bind on each side of the ball-carrier in a wedge formation. Often one or more of these team-mates is in front of the ball-carrier. This, in itself, is illegal. In any case, the 'Flying Wedge' is potentially dangerous to players who try to stop it. It is illegal.

Penalty: Penalty Kick at the place of the original infringement. (PK)

'Cavalry Charge'. The type of attack known as a 'Cavalry Charge' usually happens near the goal-line, when the attacking team is awarded a penalty kick or free kick. Attacking players form a line across the field some distance behind the kicker. These attacking players are usually a metre or two apart. At a signal from the kicker they charge forward. When they get near, the kicker tap-kicks the ball and passes it to one of them. Until the ball is kicked, the defending team must stay at least 10 metres from the mark or behind their goal-line, if that is nearer. The 'Cavalry Charge' is potentially dangerous. It is illegal.

Penalty: Penalty Kick at the place of the original infringement. (PK)

5   YELLOW & RED CARDS

(a) When a player is cautioned and temporarily suspended the referee will show that player a yellow card.

(b) When a player is sent off the referee will show that player a red card.

6   PLAYER SENT OFF

A player who is sent off takes no further part in the match.

LAW 11 – OFF-SIDE AND ON-SIDE IN GENERAL PLAY

DEFINITION

At the start of a game all players are on-side. As the match progresses players may find themselves in an off-side position. Such players are then liable to be penalised unless they become on-side again.

In general play a player is off-side if the player is in front of a team-mate who is carrying the ball or in front of a team-mate who last played the ball.

Off-side means that a player is temporarily out of the game, such players are liable to be penalised if they take part in the game.

In general play, a player can be put on-side either by an action of a team-mate or by an action of an opponent. However, the off-side player cannot be put on-side if the off-side player interferes with play; or moves forward, towards the ball, or fails to move 10 metres away from the place where the ball lands.

1 OFF-SIDE IN GENERAL PLAY

(a) A player who is in an off-side position is liable to penalty only if the player does one of three things:

Interferes with play or,
Moves forward, towards the ball or
Fails to comply with the 10 metre law (Law 11.4).

A player who is in an off-side position is not automatically penalised.

A player who receives an involuntary throw-forward is not off-side.

A player can be off-side in the in-goal.

(b) **Off-side and interfering with play.** A player who is off-side must not take part in the game. This means the player must not play the ball or obstruct an opponent.

(c) **Off-side and moving forward.** When a team-mate of an off-side player has kicked ahead, the off-side player must not move towards opponents who are waiting to play the ball, or move towards the place where the ball lands, until the player has been put on-side.

LAW 11 - OFF-SIDE AND ON-SIDE IN GENERAL PLAY

2 BEING PUT ON-SIDE BY THE ACTION OF A TEAM-MATE

In general play, there are four ways by which an off-side player can be put on-side by actions of that player or of team-mates;

(a) **Action by the player.** When the off-side player runs behind the team-mate who last kicked, touched or carried the ball, the player is put on-side.

(b) **Action by the ball-carrier.** When a team-mate carrying the ball runs in front of the off-side player, that player is put on-side.

(c) **Action by the kicker or other on-side player.** When the kicker, or team-mate who was level with or behind the kicker when (or after) the ball was kicked, runs in front of the off-side player, the player is put on-side.

(d) **When running forward,** the team-mate may be in touch or in touch-in-goal, but that team-mate must return to the playing area to put the other player on-side.

3 BEING PUT ON-SIDE BY OPPONENTS

In general play, there are three ways by which an off-side player can be put on-side by an action of the opposing team. These three ways do not apply to a player who is off-side under the 10 metre law.

(a) **Runs 5 metres with ball.** When an opponent carrying the ball runs 5 metres, the off-side player is put on-side.

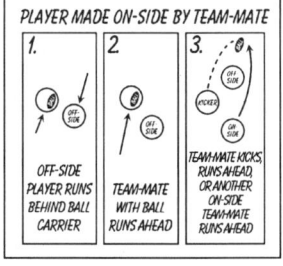

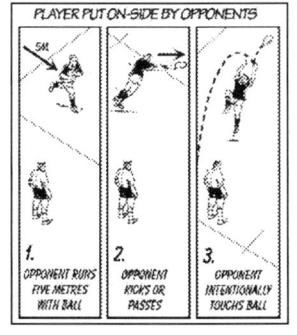

LAW 11 - OFF-SIDE AND ON-SIDE IN GENERAL PLAY

(b) **Kicks or passes.** When an opponent kicks or passes the ball, the off-side player is put on-side.

(c) **Voluntarily touches ball.** When an opponent voluntarily touches the ball but does not catch it, the off-side player is put on-side.

4 OFF-SIDE UNDER THE 10-METRE LAW

(a) When a team-mate of an off-side player has kicked ahead, the off-side player is considered to be taking part in the game if the player is in front of an imaginary line across the field which is ten metres from the opponent waiting to play the ball or from where the ball lands or may land. The off-side player must immediately move behind the imaginary 10-metre line. While moving away, the player must not obstruct an opponent. (PK)

THE TEN-METRE LAW

— 10 METRES —

(b) While moving away, the off-side player cannot be put on-side by any action of the opposing team. However, before the player has moved the full 10 metres, the player can be put on-side by any on-side team-mate who runs in front of the player.

(c) When a player who is off-side under the 10-metre law charges an opponent waiting to catch the ball, the referee blows the whistle at once and the off-side player is penalised. Delay may prove dangerous to the opponent. (PK)

(d) When a player who is off-side under the 10-metre law plays the ball which has been mis-fielded by an opponent, the off-side player is penalised. (PK)

(e) The 10-metre law is not altered by the fact that the ball has hit a goal post or a cross bar. What matters is where the ball lands. An off-side player must not be in front of the imaginary 10-metre line across the field.

LAW 11 - OFF-SIDE AND ON-SIDE IN GENERAL PLAY

(f) The 10-metre law does not apply when a player kicks the ball and an opponent charges down the kick and a team-mate of the first player who was in front of the imaginary 10-metre line across the field then plays the ball. The opponent was not 'waiting to play the ball' and the team-mate is on-side.

Penalty: When a player is penalised for being off-side in general play, the opposing team chooses either a penalty kick at the place of infringement or a scrum at the place where the offending team last played the ball. If it was last played in that team's in-goal, the scrum is formed 5 metres from the goal-line in line with where it was played.

(g) If more than one player is off-side and moving forward after a team-mate has kicked ahead, the place of infringement is the place of the off-side player closest to an opponent waiting for the ball, or closest to where the ball lands.

5 BEING PUT ON-SIDE UNDER THE 10-METRE LAW

(a) The off-side player must retire behind the 10-metre line across the field otherwise the player is liable to be penalised.

(b) While retiring, the player can be put on-side before moving behind the imaginary 10-metre line by any of the three actions of the player's teams listed above in Section 2. However, the player cannot be put on-side by any action of the opposing team.

6 ACCIDENTAL OFF-SIDE

(a) When an off-side player cannot avoid being touched by the ball or by a team-mate carrying it, the player is accidentally off-side. If the player's team gains no advantage from this, play continues. If the player's team gains an advantage, a scrum is formed with the opposing team throwing in the ball.

(b) When a player hands the ball to a team-mate in front of the first player, the receiver is off-side. Unless the receiver is considered to be voluntarily off-side (in which case a penalty kick is awarded), the receiver is accidentally off-side and a scrum is formed with the opposing team throwing in the ball.

7 OFF-SIDE AFTER A KNOCK-ON

When a player knocks-on and an off-side team-mate next plays the ball, the off-side player is liable to penalty if playing the ball prevented an opponent from gaining an advantage.

Penalty: Penalty Kick

LAW 11 - OFF-SIDE AND ON-SIDE IN GENERAL PLAY

8 OFF-SIDE AT SCRUM, RUCK, MAUL OR LINE-OUT

At a scrum, ruck, maul or line out, a player is off-side if the player is in front of the off-side line as described in the relevant parts of those laws.

9 PUTTING ON-SIDE A PLAYER RETIRING DURING A RUCK, MAUL, SCRUM OR LINE-OUT

When a ruck, maul, scrum or line-out forms, a player who is off-side and is retiring as required by law remains off-side even when the opposing team wins possession and the ruck, maul, scrum or line-out has ended.

In this situation, no action of the off-side player or team-mates can put the off-side player on-side. The off-side player can be put on-side only by the action of the opposing team. There are two such actions:

Opponent runs 5 metres with ball. When an opponent carrying the ball has run 5 metres, the off-side player is put on-side. An off-side player is not put on-side when an opponent passes the ball. Even if the opponents pass the ball several times, their action does not put the off-side player on-side.

Opponent kicks. When an opponent kicks the ball, the off-side player is put on-side.

10 LOITERING

A player who remains in an off-side position is loitering. A loiterer who prevents the opposing team from playing the ball as they wish is taking part in the game, and is penalised. The referee makes sure that the loiterer does not benefit from being put on-side by the opposing team's action.

Penalty: Penalty Kick

LAW 12 - KNOCK-ON OR THROW-FORWARD

DEFINITION - KNOCK-ON

A knock-on occurs when a player loses possession of the ball and it goes forward, or when a player hits the ball forward with the hand or arm, or when the ball hits the hand or arm and goes forward, and the ball touches the ground or another player before the original player can catch it.

'Forward' means towards the opposing team's dead-ball line.

EXCEPTION

Charge down. If the ball goes forward as in a knock-on while a player charges down an opponent's kick, but the player does not try to catch the ball, then play continues.

DEFINITION - THROW-FORWARD

A throw-forward occurs when a player throws or passes the ball forward. 'Forward' means towards the opposing team's dead-ball line.

EXCEPTION

Bounce forward. If the ball is not thrown forward but it hits a player or the ground and bounces forward, this is not a throw-forward.

LAW 12 - KNOCK-ON OR THROW-FORWARD

1 THE OUTCOME OF A KNOCK-ON OR THROW-FORWARD

(a) **Involuntary knock-on or throw-forward.** A scrum is awarded at the place of infringement.

(b) **Involuntary knock-on or throw-forward at a line-out.** A scrum is awarded 15 metres from the touch-line.

(c) **Knock-on or throw-forward into the in-goal.** If an attacking player knocks-on or throws-forward in the field-of-play and the ball goes into the opponents' in-goal and it is made dead there, a scrum is awarded where the knock-on or throw-forward happened.

(d) **Knock-on or throw-forward inside the in-goal.** If a player of either team knocks-on or throws-forward inside the in-goal, a 5-metre scrum is awarded in line with the place of infringement not closer than 5 metres from the touch-line.

(e) **Voluntary knock-on or throw-forward.** A player must not voluntarily knock-on or throw-forward.

Penalty: Penalty kick. A penalty try must be awarded if the offence prevents a try that would probably otherwise have been scored. (PK)

(f) If the ball goes forward as in a knock-on while a player attempts to catch the ball and that player catches the ball before it has touched the ground or another player, play continues.

DURING THE MATCH

In the Field-of-Play

Law 13	Kick-off and Restart Kicks
Law 14	Ball on the Ground: No Tackle
Law 15	Tackle: Ball-carrier Brought to Ground
Law 16	Ruck
Law 17	Maul
Law 18	Mark

IN THE FIELD-OF-PLAY

There are many activities in the field-of-play during a match: the kick-off (Law 13), players tackling the ball-carriers (Law 15), players going into contact with opposition players and players from their own team to form a maul (Law 17), or players going to ground to recover a ball (Law 14). After a tackle, players from both teams may stay on their feet and attempt to ruck the ball (Law 16) to maintain continuity. If the ball is kicked, a defender within that player's 22-metre area may attempt to make a mark (Law 18).

LAW 13 - KICK-OFF AND RESTART KICKS

DEFINITION

The kick-off represents the start of the match, or the restart of a match after half-time or after a score.

1 WHERE THE KICK-OFF IS TAKEN

The kick-off is taken at the centre of the half-way line. If the ball is kicked from the wrong place it is kicked-off again.

2 HOW A KICK-OFF IS TAKEN

(a) At the start of the match and after half-time, a team kicks-off with a place kick.

(b) The kicker may place the ball on sand, sawdust or a kicking tee approved by the Union.

(c) After a score a team kicks-off with a drop kick which must be taken at or behind the centre of the half-way line.

(d) If the ball is kicked-off by the wrong type of kick, it is kicked-off again.

3 WHO TAKES THE KICK-OFF

(a) At the start of the game, the team whose captain elected to take the kick after winning the toss kicks-off or the opposing team if the winning captain elected to choose end.

(b) After the half-time interval, the opponents of the team who kicked-off at the start of the game kick-off.

(c) After a score the opponents of the team who scored kick-off.

4 POSITION OF THE KICKER'S TEAM AT A KICK-OFF

All the kicker's team, except the placer, must be behind the ball when it is kicked. If they are not, a scrum is formed at the centre. Their opponents throw in the ball.

LAW 13 - KICK-OFF AND RESTART KICKS

5 POSITION OF THE OPPOSING TEAM AT A KICK-OFF

All the opposing team must stand on or behind the 10-metre line. If they are in front of that line or if they charge before the ball is kicked, it is kicked-off again.

6 KICK OFF OF 10 METRES

If the ball reaches the opponents' 10-metre line or reaches the 10-metre line and is blown back, play goes on.

7 KICK OFF OF UNDER 10 METRES BUT PLAYED BY AN OPPONENT

If the ball does not reach the opponent's 10-metre line but is first played by an opponent, play goes on.

8 KICK OFF OF UNDER 10 METRES AND NOT PLAYED BY AN OPPONENT

If the ball does not reach the opponent's 10-metre line the opposing team has two choices:

To have the ball kicked-off again, or
To have a scrum at the centre. They throw in the ball.

9 BALL GOES DIRECTLY INTO TOUCH

The ball must land in the field-of-play. If it is kicked directly into touch the opposing team has three choices:

To have the ball kicked off again, or
To have a scrum at the centre and they have the throw-in, or
To accept the kick.

LAW 13 - KICK-OFF AND RESTART KICKS

If they accept the kick, the line-out is on the half-way line. If the ball is blown behind the half-way line and goes directly into touch, the line-out is at the place where it went into touch.

10 BALL GOES INTO THE IN-GOAL

(a) If the ball is kicked into the in-goal without having touched or been touched by a player, the opposing team has three choices:

To ground the ball, or
To make it dead, or
To play on.

(b) If the opposing team grounds the ball, or if they make it dead, or if the ball becomes dead by going into touch-in-goal or on or over the dead-ball line, they have two choices:

To have a scrum formed at the centre, and they throw in the ball, or
To have the other team kick-off again.

(c) If they opt to ground the ball or make it dead, they must do so without delay. Any other action with the ball by a defending player means the player has elected to play on.

11 DROP-OUT

DEFINITION

A drop-out is used to restart play after an attacking player has put or taken the ball into the in-goal, without infringement, and a defending player has made the ball dead there or it has gone into touch-in-goal or on or over the dead-ball line.

A drop-out is a drop kick taken by the defending team. The drop-out may be taken anywhere on or behind the 22-metre line.

12 DELAY IN DROP-OUT

The drop-out must be taken without delay.

Penalty: Free kick on the 22-metre line.   (FK)

LAW 13 - KICK-OFF AND RESTART KICKS

13 DROP-OUT INCORRECTLY TAKEN

If the ball is kicked by the wrong type of kick, or from the wrong place, it must be dropped-out again.

14 DROP-OUT BALL MUST CROSS THE LINE

(a) If the ball does not cross the 22-metre line, the opposing team has two choices:

To have another drop-out, or
To have a scrum at the centre of the 22-metre line.
They throw in the ball.

(b) If the ball crosses the 22-metre line but is blown back, play continues.

(c) If the ball does not cross the 22-metre line, advantage may apply. An opponent who plays the ball can score a try.

15 BALL GOES DIRECTLY INTO TOUCH

The ball must land in the field-of-play. If it is kicked directly into touch, the opposing team has three choices:

To have another drop-out, or
To have a scrum at the centre of the 22-metre line, and they throw in the ball, or
To accept the kick. If they accept the kick, the throw-in is where the ball went into touch.

16 THE KICKER'S TEAM

(a) All the kicker's team must be behind the ball when it is kicked. If not, a scrum is formed at the centre of the 22-metre line. The opposing team throws in the ball.

(b) However, if the kick is taken so quickly that players of the kicker's team who are retiring are still in front of the ball, they will not be penalised. They must not stop retiring until they have been made on-side by an action of a team-mate. They must not take part in the game until they have been made on-side in this way.

Penalty: Scrum at the centre of the 22-metre line. The opposing team throws in the ball.

LAW 13 - KICK-OFF AND RESTART KICKS

17 THE OPPOSING TEAM

The opposing team must not charge over the 22-metre line before the ball is kicked. If they do, another drop-out is taken.

If an opponent is on the wrong side of the 22-metre line and delays or obstructs the drop-out, the player is guilty of misconduct.

Penalty: Penalty kick (PK) on the 22-metre line

LAW 14 - BALL ON THE GROUND - NO TACKLE

DEFINITION

This situation occurs when the ball is available on the ground and a player goes to ground to gather the ball, except immediately after a scrum or a ruck.

It also occurs when a player is on the ground in possession of the ball and has not been tackled.

The game is to be played by players who are on their feet. A player must not make the ball unplayable by falling down. Unplayable means that the ball is not immediately available to either team so that play may continue.

A player who makes the ball unplayable, or who obstructs the opposing team by falling down, is negating the purpose and spirit of the game and must be penalised.

A player who is not tackled, but who goes to ground while holding the ball, or a player who goes to ground and gathers the ball, must act immediately.

1 PLAYER ON THE GROUND

The player must immediately do one of three things:

Get up with the ball, or
Pass the ball, or
Release the ball.

A player who passes or releases the ball must also get up or move away from it at once. Advantage is played only if it happens immediately.

Penalty: Penalty Kick (PK)

2 WHAT THE PLAYER MUST NOT DO

Lying on or around the ball. A (PK) player must not lie on or near the ball to prevent opponents getting possession of it.

LYING NEAR THE BALL

LAW 14 - BALL ON THE GROUND - NO TACKLE

Falling over the player on the ground with the ball. A player must not voluntarily fall on or over a player with the ball who is lying on the ground. (PK)

(c) **Falling over players lying on the ground near the ball.** A player must not voluntarily fall on or over players lying on the ground with the ball between them or near them. (PK)

Penalty: Penalty Kick

DEFINITION

Near is within 1 metre.

LAW 15 - TACKLE: BALL-CARRIER BROUGHT TO THE GROUND

DEFINITION

A tackle occurs when a ball-carrier in a standing posistion is simultaneously held by one or more opponents and is brought to the ground and/or the ball touches the ground.

1   TACKLE - WHERE

A tackle can only take place in the field-of-play.

2   WHEN A TACKLE CANNOT TAKE PLACE

When the ball-carrier is held by one opponent and a team-mate binds on to that ball-carrier, a maul has been formed and a tackle cannot take place.

3   BROUGHT TO THE GROUND DEFINED

(a) If the ball-carrier has one knee or both knees on the ground, that player has been 'brought to ground'.

(b) If the ball-carrier is sitting on the ground, or on top of another player on the ground the ball carrier has been 'brought to ground'.

4   LIFTING A BALL CARRIER FROM THE GROUND

A ball-carrier who is lifted off the ground by an opponent is not tackled and play continues.

LAW 15 - TACKLE: BALL-CARRIER BROUGHT TO THE GROUND

5 THE TACKLED PLAYER

(a) A tackled player must try to make the ball available immediately so that play can continue. (PK)

(b) A tackled player must immediately pass the ball or release it. That player must also get up or move away from it at once. (PK)

(c) A tackled player may release the ball by putting it on the ground in any direction, provided this is done immediately. (PK)

(d) A tackled player may release the ball by pushing it along the ground in any direction except forward, provided this is done immediately. (PK)

(e) If a tackled player's momentum carries the player into the In-goal, the player can score a try or make a touch down. (PK)

(f) If players are tackled near to the goal-line, these players may immediately reach out and ground the ball on or over the goal-line to score a try or make a touch down. (PK)

Penalty: Penalty Kick

(g) The tackled player must not place the ball in-touch. The tackled player must not push the ball into touch. (PK)

Penalty: Penalty Kick on the 15 metre line.

6 THE TACKLER (PK)

(a) When a player tackles an opponent and they both go to ground, the tackler must immediately release the tackled player. (PK)

(b) The tackler must immediately get up or move away from the tackled player and from the ball at once. (PK)

(c) The tackler must get up before playing the ball. (PK)

Penalty: Penalty Kick

LAW 15 - TACKLE: BALL-CARRIER BROUGHT TO THE GROUND

7   AFTER A TACKLE

(a) After a tackle, all other players must be on their feet when they play the ball. Players are on their feet if no other part of their body is supported by the ground or players on the ground. (PK)

(b) After a tackle, any player lying on the ground must not prevent an opponent from getting possession of the ball. (PK)

(c) After a tackle, any player on the ground must not tackle an opponent or try to tackle an opponent. (PK)

Penalty: Penalty Kick

Exception: Ball goes into the in-goal. After a tackle near the goal-line, if the ball has been released and has gone into the in-goal any player, including a player on the ground, may ground the ball.

8   FORBIDDEN PRACTICES

(a) No player may prevent the tackled player from passing the ball. (PK)

(b) No player may prevent the tackled player from releasing the ball and getting up or moving away from it. (PK)

(c) No player may pull the ball from the tackled player before the tackled player has released it. (PK)

Penalty: Penalty Kick

Exception: An opponent may legally pull the ball from the hands or arms of a tackled player who is reaching out to ground the ball on or over the goal-line, but the opponent must not kick the ball.

(d) No player may fall on or over the tackled player. (PK)

(e) No player may fall on or over the players lying on the ground after a tackle with the ball between or near to them. (PK)

LAW 15 - TACKLE: BALL-CARRIER BROUGHT TO THE GROUND iRB

(f) Players on their feet must not charge or obstruct an opponent who is (PK) not near the ball.

Penalty: Penalty Kick

(g) **Danger:** Failure to pass or release. Danger may arise if a tackled (PK) player fails to release the ball or move away from it immediately, or if that player is prevented from so doing. If either of these happens the referee awards a penalty kick immediately.

Penalty: Penalty Kick

9   DOUBT ABOUT FAILURE TO COMPLY

If the ball becomes unplayable at a tackle and there is doubt about which player did not conform to law, the referee orders a scrum immediately with the throw-in by the team that was moving forward prior to the stoppage or, if no team was moving forward, by the attacking team.

LAW 16 - RUCK

LAW 16 - RUCK

DEFINITIONS

A ruck is a phase of play where one or more players from each team, who are on their feet, in physical contact, close around the ball on the ground. Open play has ended.

Rucking. Players are rucking when they are in a ruck and using their feet to try to win or keep possession of the ball, without being guilty of foul play.

1   FORMING A RUCK

Where A ruck can take place only in the field-of-play.

How Players are on their feet. At least one player must be in physical contact with an opponent.

SUMMARY

Ruck: Ball on the ground; needs at least two players on their feet, one from each team.

2   JOINING A RUCK

(a) All players forming, joining or taking part in a ruck must have their heads and shoulders no lower than their hips. (FK)

   Penalty: Free Kick

(b) A player joining a ruck must bind onto the ruck with at least one arm around the body of a team-mate, using the whole arm. (PK)

(c) Placing a hand on another player in the ruck does not constitute binding. (PK)

(d) All players forming, joining or taking part in a ruck must be on their feet. (PK)

   Penalty: Penalty Kick

LAW 16 - RUCK

3 RUCKING

(a) Players in a ruck must endeavour to stay on their feet.

(b) A player must not voluntarily fall or kneel in a ruck. This is dangerous play. (PK)

(c) A player must not voluntarily collapse a ruck. This is dangerous play. (PK)

(d) A player must not jump on top of a ruck. (PK)

Penalty: Penalty Kick

(e) Players must have their heads and shoulders no lower than their hips. (PK)

Penalty: Free Kick

(f) A player rucking for the ball must not ruck players on the ground. A player rucking for the ball tries to step over players on the ground and must not voluntarily step on them. A player rucking must do so near the ball. (PK)

Penalty: Penalty Kick for dangerous play

4 OTHER RUCK OFFENCES

(a) Players must not return the ball into a ruck. (FK)

Penalty: Free Kick

(b) Players must not handle the ball in a ruck. (PK)

(c) Players must not pick up the ball in a ruck with their legs. (PK)

(d) Players on the ground in or near the ruck must try to move away from the ball. These players must not interfere with the ball in the ruck or as it comes out of the ruck. (PK)

(e) A player must not fall on or over a ball as it is coming out of a ruck. (PK)

Penalty: Penalty Kick

(f) A player must not take any action to make the opponents think that the ball is out of the ruck while it is still in the ruck. (FK)

Penalty: Free Kick

LAW 16 - RUCK

5 OFF-SIDE AT THE RUCK

(a) **The off-side line.** There are two off-side lines parallel to the goal-lines, one for each team. Each off-side line runs through the hindmost foot of the hindmost player in the ruck.

(b) Players must either join a ruck, or retire behind the off-side line immediately. If a player loiters at the side of a ruck, the player is off-side. (PK)

(c) **Players joining the ruck.** All players joining a ruck must do so from behind the foot of the hindmost team-mate in the ruck. A player may join alongside this hindmost player. If the player joins the ruck from the opponents' side, or in front of the hindmost team-mate, the player is off-side. (PK)

Penalty: Penalty Kick on the offending team's off-side line

(d) **Players not joining the ruck.** If a player is in front of the off-side line and does not join the ruck, the player must retire behind the off-side line at once. If a player who is behind the off-side line oversteps it and does not join the ruck the player is off-side. (PK)

Penalty: Penalty Kick on the offending team's off-side line

(e) **Players leaving or rejoining the ruck.** If a player leaves a ruck that player must immediately retire behind the off-side line otherwise the player is off-side. Once the player is on-side, the player may rejoin the ruck. If the player rejoins in front of the hindmost team-mate in the ruck, the player is off-side. The player may rejoin the ruck alongside the hindmost team-mate. (PK)

Penalty: Penalty Kick on the offending team's off-side line

RUCK AND MAUL OFF-SIDE
AT A RUCK OR MAUL, THE OFF-SIDE LINE RUNS THROUGH THE HIND MOST FOOT OF THE PLAYER OF THE SAME TEAM. THE PLAYER MARKED WITH CROSS IS OFF-SIDE.

LAW 16 - RUCK

6 SUCCESSFUL END TO A RUCK

A ruck ends successfully when the ball leaves the ruck, or when the ball is on or over the goal-line.

7 UNSUCCESSFUL END TO A RUCK

(a) A ruck ends unsuccessfully when the ball becomes unplayable and a scrum is ordered.

The team that was moving forward immediately before the ball became unplayable in the ruck throws in the ball.

If neither team was moving forward, or if the referee cannot decide which team was moving forward before the ball became unplayable in the ruck, the team that was moving forward before the ruck began throws in the ball.

If neither team was moving forward, then the attacking team throws in the ball.

(b) Before the referee blows the whistle for a scrum, the referee allows a reasonable amount of time for the ball to emerge, especially if either team is moving forward. If the ruck stops moving, or if the referee decides that the ball will probably not emerge within a reasonable time, the referee must order a scrum.

LAW 17 - MAUL

DEFINITION

A maul occurs when a player carrying the ball is held by one or more opponents, and one or more of the ball-carrier's team-mates bind on the ball-carrier. All the players involved are on their feet and moving towards a goal-line. Open play has ended.

1 FORMING A MAUL

Where A maul only takes place in the field-of-play.

How Players must be on their feet.

Summary

Maul: At least three players; all on their feet, the ball-carrier and one from each team.

2 JOINING A MAUL

(a) Players joining a maul must have their heads and shoulders no lower than their hips. (FK)

Penalty: Free Kick

(b) A player must be caught in or bound to the maul and not just alongside it. (PK)

(c) Placing a hand on another player in the maul does not constitute binding. (PK)

Penalty: Penalty Kick

(d) **Keeping players on their feet.** Players in a maul must endeavour to stay on their feet. The ball carrier in a maul may go to ground providing the ball is available immediately and play continues. (PK)

LAW 17 - MAUL

(e) A player must not voluntarily collapse a maul. This is dangerous play. (PK)

(f) A player must not jump on top of a maul. (PK)

Penalty: Penalty Kick

3 OTHER MAUL OFFENCES

(a) A player must not try to drag an opponent out of a maul. (PK)

Penalty: Penalty Kick

(b) A player must not take any action to make the opposing team think that (FK) the ball is out of the maul while it is still in the maul.

Penalty: Free Kick

4 OFF-SIDE AT THE MAUL

(a) **The off-side line.** There are two off-side lines parallel to the goal-lines, one for each team. Each off-side line runs through the hindmost foot of the hindmost player in the maul.

(b) A player must either join a maul, or retire behind the off-side line (PK) immediately. If a player loiters at the side of a maul, the player is off-side.

Penalty: Penalty Kick on the offending team's off-side line

(c) **Players joining the maul.** Players joining a maul must do so from (PK) behind the foot of the hindmost team-mate in the maul. The player may join alongside this player. If the player joins the maul from the opponents' side, or in front of the hindmost team-mate, the player is off-side.

Penalty: Penalty Kick on the offending team's off-side line

(d) **Players not joining the maul.** All players in front of the off-side line (PK) and who do not join the maul, must retire behind the off-side line at once. A player who does not do so, is off-side. If any player who is behind the off-side line oversteps it and does not join the maul, the player is off-side.

Penalty: Penalty Kick on the offending team's off-side line

LAW 17 - MAUL

(e) **Players leaving or rejoining the maul.** (PK) Players who leave a maul must immediately retire behind the off-side line, otherwise, they are off-side. If the player rejoins the maul in front of the hindmost team-mate in the maul, they are off-side. The player may rejoin the maul alongside the hindmost team-mate.

Penalty: Penalty Kick on the offending team's off-side line.

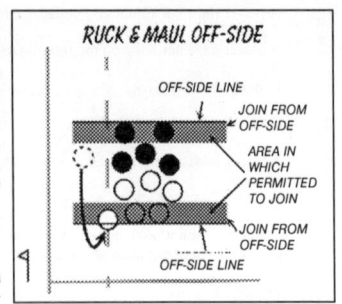

RUCK & MAUL OFF-SIDE

OFF-SIDE LINE
JOIN FROM OFF-SIDE
AREA IN WHICH PERMITTED TO JOIN
JOIN FROM OFF-SIDE
OFF-SIDE LINE

5 SUCCESSFUL END TO A MAUL

A maul ends successfully when the ball leaves the maul or a player with the ball leaves the maul. The maul ends when the ball is on or over the goal-line.

6 UNSUCCESSFUL END TO A MAUL

(a) A maul ends unsuccessfully if the ball in the maul remains stationary or stops moving forward and a scrum is ordered.

(b) A maul ends unsuccessfully if the ball becomes unplayable or collapses (not as a result of foul play) and a scrum is ordered.

(c) **Scrum following maul.** The ball is thrown in by the team not in possession when the maul began. If the referee cannot decide which team had possession, the team moving forward before the maul stopped moving forward throws in the ball. If neither team was moving forward, the attacking team throws in the ball.

(d) When a maul remains stationary or stops moving forward but the ball is being moved and the referee can see it, a reasonable time is allowed for the ball to emerge. If it does not emerge within a reasonable time a scrum is ordered.

(e) Once a maul has stopped moving forward it must not start moving again. A scrum is ordered.

LAW 17 - MAUL

(f) When the ball in a maul becomes unplayable, the referee does not allow prolonged wrestling for it. A scrum is ordered.

(g) If the ball-carrier in a maul goes to ground, including being on one or both knees or sitting, the referee orders a scrum unless the ball is immediately available.

(h) **Scrum after a maul when catcher is held.** If a player catches the ball direct from an opponent's kick, except from a kick-off or a drop-out, and the player is immediately held by an opponent, a maul may form. Then if the maul remains stationary, stops moving forward, or if the ball becomes unplayable, and a scrum is ordered, the team of the ball catcher throws in the ball.

'Direct from an opponent's kick' means the ball did not touch another player or the ground before the player caught it.

If a maul moves into the player's in-goal, where the ball is touched down or becomes unplayable, a 5-metre scrum is formed. The attacking team throws in the ball.

LAW 18 - MARK

DEFINITION

To make a mark, a player must be on or behind that player's 22 metre line. A player with one foot on the 22 metre line or behind it is considered to be 'in the 22'. The player must make a clean catch direct from an opponent's kick and at the same time shout "Mark!"

A mark cannot be made from a kick-off.

A kick is awarded for a mark. The place for the kick is the place of the mark.

A player may make a mark even though the ball touched a goal post or crossbar before being caught.

A player from the defending team may make a mark in in-goal.

1   AFTER A MARK

The referee immediately blows the whistle and awards a kick to the player who made the mark.

2   KICK AWARDED

The kick is awarded at the place of the mark.

3   KICK - WHERE

The kick is taken at or behind the mark on a line through the mark.

4   WHO KICKS

The kick is taken by the player who made the mark. If that player cannot take the kick within one minute, a scrum is formed at the place of the mark with the ball thrown in by the player's team. If the mark is in the in-goal, the scrum is 5 metres from the goal-line, on a line through the mark.

LAW 18 - MARK

5 HOW THE KICK IS TAKEN

The provisions of Law 21 - Free Kicks - apply to a kick awarded after a mark.

6 SCRUM ALTERNATIVE

(a) The team of the player who made the mark may choose to take a scrum.

(b) **Where the scrum is.** If the mark is in the field-of-play, the scrum is at the place of the mark, but at least 5 metres from the touch-line. If the mark is in-goal, the scrum is 5 metres from the goal-line on a line through the mark, and at least 5 metres from the touch-line.

(c) **Who throws in.** The team of the player who made the mark throws the ball in.

7 PENALTY KICK AWARDED

(a) An opponent, whether on-side or off-side, must not charge a player who has made a mark after the referee has blown the whistle.　(PK)

Penalty: Penalty Kick

(b) **Where penalty kick is taken.** If the infringing player is on-side, the penalty kick is taken at the place of the infringement. If the infringing player is off-side, the penalty kick is taken at the place of the off-side line (Law 11 Off-side and On-side in General Play.)

(c) **The penalty kick.** Any player from the non-offending team may take the penalty kick.

DURING THE MATCH

RESTARTS

Law 19	Touch, Line-out and Line-out Off-side
Law 20	Scrum
Law 21	Penalty and Free Kicks

DURING THE MATCH – RESTARTS

RESTARTING THE GAME AFTER THE BALL HAS BEEN MADE DEAD

There are four methods of restarting the game after the ball has been made dead; these are detailed in the next three laws. The line-out (Law 19) is used to restart the game after the ball has gone into touch. The scrum (Law 20) is used to restart the game after some infringements whilst penalty kicks and free kicks (Law 21) are used to restart the game after other infringements.

LAW 19 - TOUCH, LINE-OUT AND LINE-OUT OFF-SIDE

DEFINITIONS

'Kicked directly into touch' means that the ball was kicked into touch without landing on the playing area, and without touching a player or the referee.

'The 22' is the area between the goal-line and the 22-metre line, including the 22-metre line but excluding the goal-line.

The line-of-touch is an imaginary line in the field-of-play at right angles to the touch-line through the place where the ball is thrown in.

The ball is in touch when it is not being carried by a player and it touches the touch-line or anything or anyone on or beyond the touch-line.

The ball is in touch when a player is carrying it and the ball-carrier (or the ball) touches the touch-line or the ground beyond the touch-line.

The place where the ball-carrier (or the ball) touched or crossed the touch-line is where it went into touch.

The ball is in-touch if a player catches the ball and that player has a foot on the touch-line or the ground beyond the touch-line.

If a player has one foot in the field of play and one foot in touch and holds the ball, the ball is in touch.

If the ball crosses the touch-line or touch-in-goal line, and is caught by a player who has both feet in the playing area, the ball is not in touch or touch-in-goal. Such a player may knock the ball into the playing area. If a player jumps and catches the ball, both feet must land in the playing area otherwise the ball is in touch or touch-in-goal.

A player in touch may kick or knock the ball, but not hold it, provided it has not crossed the plane of the touch-line. The plane of the touch-line is the vertical space rising immediately above the touch-line.

80

LAW 19 - TOUCH, LINE-OUT AND LINE-OUT OFF-SIDE

1 THROW-IN

NO GAIN IN GROUND

(a) **Outside a team's 22, a team member kicks directly into touch.** Except for a penalty kick, when a player anywhere in the playing area who is outside the 22 kicks directly into touch, there is no gain in ground. The throw-in is taken either at the place opposite where the player kicked the ball, or at the place where it went into touch, whichever is nearer that player's goal-line.

(b) **Player takes ball into that team's 22.** When a defending player gets the ball outside the 22, takes or puts it inside the 22, and then kicks directly into touch, there is no gain in ground.

GAIN IN GROUND

(c) **Player inside that team's 22.** When a defending player gets the ball inside the 22, or that player's in-goal and kicks to touch, the throw-in is where the ball went into touch.

(d) **Kicks indirectly into touch.** When a player anywhere in the playing area kicks indirectly into touch, so that the ball first bounces in the field-of-play, the throw-in is taken where the ball went into touch.

(e) **Penalty kick.** When a player kicks to touch from a penalty kick anywhere in the playing area, the throw-in is taken where the ball went into touch.

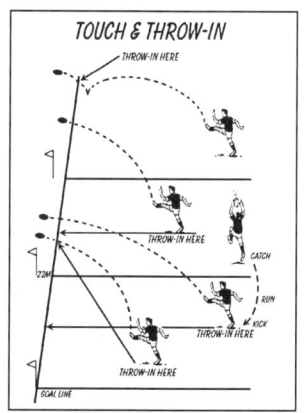

FREE KICK

(f) **Outside the kicker's 22, no gain in ground.** When a free kick awarded outside the 22 goes directly into touch, the throw-in is in line with where the ball was kicked, or where it went into touch, whichever is nearer the kicker's goal-line.

81

LAW 19 - TOUCH, LINE-OUT AND LINE-OUT OFF-SIDE

(g) **Inside the kicker's 22 or in-goal, gain in ground.** When a free kick is awarded in the 22 or in-goal and the kick goes directly into touch, the throw-in is where the ball went into touch.

2 QUICK THROW-IN

(a) A player may take a quick throw-in without waiting for a line-out to form.

(b) For a quick throw-in, the player may be anywhere outside the field of play between the place where the ball went into touch and the player's goal-line.

(c) A player must not take a quick throw-in after the line-out has formed. If the player does, the quick throw-in is disallowed. The same team throws in at the line-out.

(d) For a quick throw-in, the player must use the ball that went into touch. If, after it went to touch and was made dead, another ball is used, or if another person has touched the ball apart from the player throwing it in, then the quick throw-in is disallowed. The same team throws in at the line-out.

(e) At a quick throw-in, if the player does not throw the ball in straight so that it travels at least 5 metres along the line-of-touch before it touches the ground or another player, or if the player steps into the field-of-play when the ball is thrown, then the quick throw-in is disallowed. The opposing team chooses to throw in at either a line-out where the quick throw-in was attempted, or a scrum on the 15-metre line at that place. If they too throw in the ball incorrectly at the line-out, a scrum is formed on the 15-metre line. The team that first threw in the ball throws in the ball at the scrum.

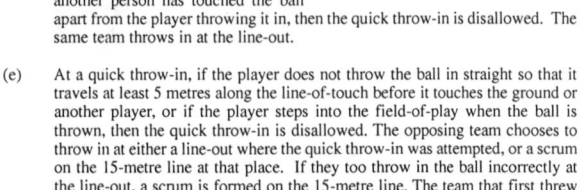

(f) At a quick throw-in, a player may come to the line-of-touch and leave without being penalised.

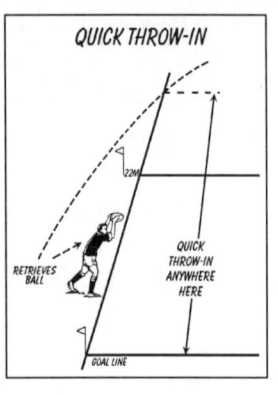

LAW 19 - TOUCH, LINE-OUT AND LINE-OUT OFF-SIDE

(g) At a quick throw-in, a player must not prevent the ball being thrown in 5 metres. **(FK)**

Penalty: Free Kick on 15-metre line

(h) If a player carrying the ball is forced into touch, that player must release the ball to an opposition player so that there can be a quick throw-in. **(PK)**

Penalty: Penalty Kick on 15-metre line

3 OTHER THROW-INS

On all other occasions, the throw-in is taken where the ball went into touch.

4 WHO THROWS-IN

The throw-in is taken by an opponent of the player who last held or touched the ball before it went into touch. When there is doubt, the attacking team takes the throw-in.

Exception

When a team takes a penalty kick, and the ball is kicked into touch, the throw-in is taken by a player of the team that took the penalty kick. This applies whether the ball was kicked directly or indirectly to touch.

5 HOW THE THROW-IN IS TAKEN

The player taking the throw-in must stand at the correct place. The player must not step into the field-of-play when the ball is thrown. The ball must be thrown straight, so that it travels at least 5 metres along the line-of-touch before it first touches the ground or touches or is touched by a player.

LAW 19 - TOUCH, LINE-OUT AND LINE-OUT OFF-SIDE

6 INCORRECT THROW-IN

(a) If the throw-in at a line-out is incorrect, the opposing team has the choice of throwing in at a line-out or a scrum on the 15-metre line. If they choose the throw-in to the line-out and it is again incorrect, a scrum is formed. The team that took the first throw-in throws in the ball.

(b) The throw-in at the line-out must be taken without delay and without pretending to throw. (FK)

Penalty: Free Kick on the 15-metre line

(c) A player must not voluntarily or repeatedly throw the ball in not straight. (PK)

Penalty: Penalty Kick on the 15-metre line

LAW 19 - TOUCH, LINE-OUT AND LINE-OUT OFF-SIDE

LINE-OUT

DEFINITIONS

The purpose of the line-out is to restart play, quickly, safely and fairly, after the ball has gone into touch, with a throw-in between two lines of players.

Line-out players. Line-out players are the players who form the two lines that make a line-out.

Receiver. The receiver is the player in position to catch the ball when line-out players pass or knock the ball back from the line-out. Any player may be the receiver but each team may have only one receiver at a line-out.

Players taking part in the line-out known as participating players. Players taking part in the line-out are the player who throws-in and an immediate opponent, the two players waiting to receive the ball from the line-out and the line-out players.

All other players. All other players who are not taking part in the line-out must be at least 10 metres behind the line-of-touch, on or behind their goal-line if that is nearer, until the line-out ends.

15-metre line. The 15-metre line is 15 metres in-field and parallel with the touch-line.

Scrum after line-out. Any scrum ordered because of an infringement or stoppage at the line-out is on the 15-metre line on the line-of-touch

7 FORMING A LINE-OUT

(a) **Minimum.** At least two players from each team must form a line-out. (FK)

(b) **Maximum.** The team throwing in the ball decides the maximum number of players in the line-out. (FK)

(c) The opposing team may have fewer line-out players but they must not have more. (FK)

(d) When the ball is in touch, every player who approaches the line-of-touch is presumed to do so to form a line-out. (FK)

(e) If the team throwing in the ball put fewer than the usual number of players in the line-out, their opponents must be given a reasonable time to move enough players out of the line-out to satisfy this law. (FK)

LAW 19 - TOUCH, LINE-OUT AND LINE-OUT OFF-SIDE

(f) These players must leave the line-out without delay. They must move to the off-side line, 10 metres behind the line-of-touch. If the line-out ends before they reach this line, they may rejoin play. **(FK)**

(g) **Failure to form a line-out.** A team must not voluntarily fail to form a line-out. **(FK)**

(h) **Where the line-out players must stand.** **(FK)** The front of the line-out is not less than 5 metres from the touch-line. The back of the line-out is not more than 15 metres from the touch-line. All line-out players must stand between these two points.

(i) **Two single straight lines.** **(FK)** The line-out players of both teams form two single parallel lines each at right angles to the touch-line.

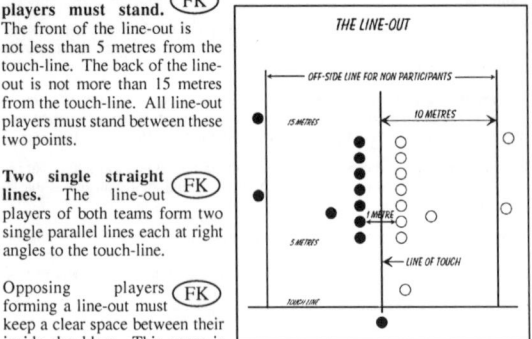

(j) Opposing players **(FK)** forming a line-out must keep a clear space between their inside shoulders. This space is determined when players are in an upright stance.

THE LINE-OUT

- OFF-SIDE LINE FOR NON PARTICIPANTS -
- 15 METRES
- 10 METRES
- 1 METRE
- 5 METRES
- LINE OF TOUCH
- TOUCH LINE

(k) **Metre gap.** Each line of players must be half a metre on their side of the line-of-touch. **(PK)**

Penalty: (a) - (k) Free Kick on the 15-metre line

(l) The line-of-touch must not be within five etres of the goal-line.

(m) After the line-out has formed, but before the ball has been thrown in, a player must not hold, push, charge into, or obstruct an opponent. **(PK)**

Penalty: Penalty Kick on the 15-metre line

LAW 19 - TOUCH, LINE-OUT AND LINE-OUT OFF-SIDE

8 BEGINNING AND ENDING A LINE-OUT

(a) **Line-out begins.** The line-out begins when the ball leaves the hands of the player throwing it in.

(b) **Line-out ends.** The line-out ends when the ball or a player carrying it leaves the line-out.

This includes the following:

When the ball is thrown, knocked or kicked out of the line-out, the line-out ends.

When a line-out player hands the ball to a player who is peeling-off, the line-out ends.

When the ball is thrown beyond the 15-metre line, or when a player takes or puts it beyond that line, the line-out ends.

When a ruck or maul develops in a line-out, and all the feet of all the players in the ruck or maul move beyond the line-of-touch, the line-out ends.

When the ball becomes unplayable in a line-out, the line-out ends. Play restarts with a scrum.

9 OPTIONS AVAILABLE IN A LINE-OUT

(a) **Off-side.** A line-out player must not be off-side. The off-side line runs through the line-of-touch until the ball is thrown in. After the ball has touched a player or the ground, the off-side line is a line through the ball.

Penalty: Penalty Kick on the 15-metre line (PK)

(b) Players jumping for the ball may take a step in any direction providing they do not step across the line-of-touch.

Penalty: Penalty Kick on the 15-metre line (PK)

(c) **Levering on an opponent.** A line-out player must not use an opponent as a support when jumping.

Penalty: Penalty Kick on the 15-metre line (PK)

LAW 19 - TOUCH, LINE-OUT AND LINE-OUT OFF-SIDE

(d) **Holding or shoving.** A line-out player must not hold, push, charge, obstruct or grasp an opponent not holding the ball except when a ruck or maul is taking place. (FK)

   Penalty: Penalty Kick on the 15-metre line

(e) **Illegal charging.** A line-out player must not charge an opponent except in an attempt to tackle the opponent or to play the ball. (FK)

   Penalty: Penalty Kick on the 15-metre line

(f) **Levering on a team-mate.** A jumping line-out player must not use a team-mate as a support to jump. (FK)

   Penalty: Free Kick on the 15-metre line

(g) **Lifting.** A line-out player must not lift a team-mate. (FK)

   Penalty: Free Kick on the 15-metre line

(h) **Support before jumping.** A player must not support a team-mate before the team-mate has jumped. (FK)

   Penalty: Free Kick on the 15-metre line

LAW 19 - TOUCH, LINE-OUT AND LINE-OUT OFF-SIDE

(i) **Jumping or supporting before the ball is thrown.** (FK)
A player must not jump for the ball or support any player before the ball has left the hands of the player throwing it in.

Penalty: Free Kick on the 15-metre line

(j) **Support below the waist.** A player must not support a jumping team-mate below the waist. (PK)

Penalty: Penalty Kick on the 15-metre line

(k) **Blocking the throw-in.** A line-out player must not stand less than 5 metres from the touch-line. A line-out player must not prevent the ball being thrown in 5 metres. (FK)

Penalty: Free Kick on the 15-metre line

(l) When the ball has been thrown beyond a player in the line-out, that player may move to the space between the touch-line and the 5 metres mark. If the player moves into that space the player must not move towards that player's goal-line before the line-out ends, except in a peeling off movement. (FK)

Penalty: Free-Kick on the 15-metre line

(m) Catching or deflecting. When jumping for the ball, a player must use either both hands or the inside arm to try to catch or deflect the ball. The jumper must not use the outside arm alone to try to catch or deflect the ball. (FK)

If the jumper has both hands above the head either hand may be used to play the ball.

Penalty: Free Kick on the 15-metre line.

LAW 19 - TOUCH, LINE-OUT AND LINE-OUT OFF-SIDE **iRB**

10 OPTIONS AVAILABLE TO PLAYERS NOT IN THE LINE-OUT

In general, a player not taking part in a line-out must stay at least 10 metres behind the line-of-touch, or on or behind that player's goal-line if that is nearer, until the line-out ends.

There are two exceptions to this:

Exception 1: Long throw-in. If the player who is throwing in throws the ball beyond the 15-metre line, a player of the same team may run forward to take the ball. If that player does so, an opponent may also run forward. (PK)

Penalty: Penalty Kick on the offending team's off-side line, opposite the place of infringement but not less than 15 metres from the touch-line.

Exception 2: Receiver runs into a gap. A receiver may run into a gap in the line-out and take the ball. The receiver must not charge or obstruct an opponent in the line-out during such action. (PK)

Penalty: Penalty Kick on the 15-metre line

11 PEELING OFF

DEFINITION

A line-out player 'peels off' when leaving the line-out to catch the ball knocked or passed back by a team-mate. Except for peeling off or joining a ruck or maul, a line-out player must not leave the line-out until it ends.

(a) **When:** A player must not peel off until the ball has left the hands of the player throwing it in. (FK)

(b) **Where:** A player who peels off, must stay near the line-out and move parallel with it until the line-out ends or a ruck or maul is formed and that player joins it. (FK)

Penalty: Free Kick on the 15-metre line

(c) Players may change their positions in the line-out before the ball is thrown in.

LAW 19 - TOUCH, LINE-OUT AND LINE-OUT OFF-SIDE

12 OFF-SIDE AT THE LINE-OUT

(a) When a line-out forms, there are two separate off-side lines, parallel to the goal-lines, for the teams.

(b) **Participating players.** One off-side line applies to the players taking part in the line-out (usually some or all of the forwards, plus the scrum-half and the player throwing in). Until the ball is thrown in, and has touched a player or the ground, this off-side line is the line-of-touch. After that, the off-side line is a line through the ball.

(c) **Players not taking part.** The other off-side line applies to the players not taking part in the line-out (usually the backs). For them, the off-side line is 10 metres behind the line-of-touch or their goal line, *if that is nearer.*

The line-out off-side law is different in the case of a long throw-in, or in the case of a ruck or maul in the line-out.

13 OFF-SIDE WHEN TAKING PART IN THE LINE-OUT

(a) **Before the ball has touched a player or the ground.** A player must (PK) not overstep the line-of-touch. A player is off-side, if, before the ball has touched a player or the ground, that player oversteps the line-of-touch, unless doing so while jumping for the ball. The player must jump from that player's side of the line-of-touch.

Penalty: Penalty Kick on the 15-metre line

(b) If a player jumps and crosses the line-of-touch but fails to catch the ball, that player is not penalised provided that player gets back on-side without delay.

(c) **After the ball has touched a player or the ground.** A player not (PK) carrying the ball is off-side if, after the ball has touched a player or the ground, that player steps in front of the ball, unless tackling (or trying to tackle) an opponent. Any attempt to tackle must start from that player's side of the ball.

(d) The referee must penalise any player who, voluntarily or not, moves (PK) into an off-side position without trying to win possession or tackle an opponent.

Penalty: Penalty Kick on the 15-metre line

LAW 19 - TOUCH, LINE-OUT AND LINE-OUT OFF-SIDE

14 PLAYER THROWING-IN

There are four options available to the player throwing-in (and the thrower's immediate opponent):

(a) The thrower may stay within 5 metres of the touch-line.

(b) The thrower may retire to the off-side line 10 metres behind the line-of-touch.

(c) The thrower may join the line-out as soon as the ball has been thrown 5 metres.

(d) The thrower may move into the receiver position if that position is empty.

If the thrower goes anywhere else, the thrower is off-side.

Penalty: Penalty Kick on the 15-metre line (PK)

15 OFF-SIDE WHEN NOT TAKING PART IN THE LINE-OUT

(a) **Before the line-out has ended.** The off-side line is 10 metres behind the line-of-touch, or the player's goal-line, whichever is nearer.

A player who is not taking part in the line-out is offside if that player oversteps the off-side line before the line-out has ended. (PK)

Penalty: Penalty Kick on the offending team's off-side line opposite the place of infringement, at least 15 metres from the touch-line.

(b) Players not yet on-side when the ball is thrown in. A player may throw in the ball even if a team-mate has not yet reached the off-side line. (PK) However, if this player is not trying to reach an on-side position without delay, this player is off-side.

Penalty: Penalty Kick on the offending team's off-side line opposite the place of infringement, at least 15 metres from the touch-line

Exception: Long throw-in. There is an exception to the law of off-side at the line-out. It applies if the ball is thrown beyond the 15-metre line. As soon as the ball leaves the hands of the player throwing in, any players of the thrower's team may run for the ball.

LAW 19 - TOUCH, LINE-OUT AND LINE-OUT OFF-SIDE

This means that a player taking part in the line-out may run in-field beyond the 15-metre line, and a player not taking part in the line-out may run forward across the off-side line.

If this happens, an opponent may also run in-field or run forward.

However, if a player runs in-field or runs forward to take a long throw-in, and the ball is not thrown beyond the 15-metre line, this player is off-side and must be penalised. (PK)

Penalty: Penalty Kick

For players taking part in the line-out: penalty kick is on the 15-metre line.

For players not taking part in the line-out: penalty kick is on the offending team's off-side line at the place of infringement, at least 15 metres from the touch-line.

16 OFF-SIDE AT RUCKS OR MAULS IN THE LINE-OUT

(a) When a ruck or a maul develops in a line-out, the off-side line for a player taking part in the line-out no longer runs through the ball. The off-side line is now the hindmost foot of that player's team in the ruck or maul.

(b) However, for players not taking part in the line-out, the off-side line is still 10 metres behind the line-of-touch. For these players, the line-out does not end when a ruck or maul develops.

(c) It ends when the ruck or maul leaves the line-of-touch. For this to happen, all the feet of all the players in the ruck or maul must have left the line-of-touch.

(d) A player taking part in the line-out must either join the ruck or maul, (PK) or retire to the off-side line and stay at that line. Otherwise that player is off-side.

Penalty: Penalty Kick on the 15-metre line

(e) The rest of the law of ruck or maul applies. A player must not join the (PK) ruck or maul from the opponents' side.

Players must not join it in front of the off-side line. If they do, they are off-side.

Penalty: Penalty Kick on the 15-metre line

LAW 20 - SCRUM

(f) **Players not taking part in the line-out.** When a ruck or maul develops in a line-out, the line-out has not ended until all the feet of all the players in the ruck or maul have moved beyond the line-of-touch. (PK)

Until then, the off-side line for players not taking part in the line-out is still 10 metres behind the line-of-touch, or the goal-line if that is nearer. A player who oversteps this off-side line is off-side.

Penalty: Penalty Kick on the off-side line at least 15 metres from the touch-line.

LAW 20 - SCRUM

LAW 20 - SCRUM

DEFINITIONS

The purpose of the scrum is to restart play quickly, safely and fairly, after a minor infringement or a stoppage.

A scrum is formed in the field-of-play when eight players from each team, bound together in three rows for each team, close up with their opponents so that the heads of the front rows are interlocked. This creates a tunnel into which a scrum-half throws in the ball so that front-row players can compete for possession by hooking the ball with either of their feet.

The tunnel is the space between the two front rows.

The player of either team who throws the ball into the scrum is the scrum-half.

The middle line is an imaginary line on the ground in the tunnel beneath the line where the shoulders of the two front rows meet.

The middle player in each front row is the hooker.

The players on either side of the hooker are the props. The left-side props are the loose-head props. The right-side props are the tight-head props.

The two players in the second row who shove on the props and the hooker are the locks.

The outside players who bind onto the second or third row are the flankers.

The player in the third row who usually pushes on both locks is the No.8. Alternatively, the No. 8 may shove on a lock and a flanker.

1 FORMING A SCRUM

(a) **Where the scrum takes place.** The place for a scrum is where the infringement or stoppage happened, or as near to it as is practicable in the field-of-play, unless otherwise stated in law.

(b) If this is less than 5 metres from a touch-line, the place for the scrum is 5 metres from that touch-line. A scrum can take place only in the field-of-play. The middle line of the scrum must not be within 5 metres of the goal-line when it is formed.

LAW 20 - SCRUM

(c) If there is an infringement or stoppage in in-goal, the place for the scrum is 5 metres from the goal-line.

(d) The scrum is formed in line with the place of the infringement or stoppage.

(e) **No delay.** A team must not voluntarily delay forming a scrum. (FK)

Penalty: Free Kick

(f) **Number of players: eight.** A scrum must have eight players from each team. All eight players must stay bound to the scrum until it ends. Each front row must have three players in it, no more and no less. Two locks must form the second row. (PK)

Penalty: Penalty Kick

Exception : When a team is reduced to fewer than fifteen for any reason, then the number of players of each team in the scrum may be similarly reduced. Where a permitted reduction is made by one team, there is no requirement for the other team to make a similar reduction. However, a team must not have fewer than five players in the scrum. (PK)

Penalty: Penalty Kick

(g) **Front rows coming together.** First, the referee marks with a foot the place where the scrum is to be formed. Before the two front rows come together they must be standing not more than an arm's length apart. The ball is in the scrum-half's hands, ready to be thrown in. The front rows must crouch so that when they meet, each player's head and shoulders are no lower than the hips. The front rows must interlock so that no player's head is next to the head of a team-mate. (FK)

(h) The front-rows crouch and pause, and then come together only when the referee calls 'engage'. This call is not a command but an indication that the front rows may come together when ready. (FK)

Penalty: Free Kick

(i) A crouched position is the extension of the normal stance by bending the knees sufficiently to move into the engagement without a charge.

(j) **Charging.** A front row must not form at a distance from its opponents and rush against them. This is dangerous play. (PK)

Penalty: Penalty Kick

LAW 20 - SCRUM

(k) **Stationary and parallel.** Until the ball leaves the scrum-half's hands, the scrum must be stationary and the middle line must be parallel to the goal-lines. A team must not shove the scrum away from the mark before the ball is thrown in. (FK)

Penalty: Free Kick

2 FRONT-ROW PLAYERS' POSITIONS

(a) **All players in a position to shove.** When a scrum has formed, the body and feet of each front-row player must be in a normal position to make a forward shove. (FK)

(b) This means that the front-row players must have both feet on the ground, with their weight firmly on at least one foot. Players must not cross their feet, although the foot of one player may cross a team-mate's foot. Each player's shoulders must be no lower than the hips. (FK)

Penalty: Free Kick

(c) **Hooker in a position to hook.** Until the ball is thrown in, a hooker must be in a position to hook the ball. The hookers must have both feet on the ground, with their weight firmly on at least one foot. A hooker's foremost foot must not be in front of the foremost foot of that team's props. (FK)

Penalty: Free Kick

3 BINDING IN THE SCRUM

DEFINITION

When a player binds on a team-mate that player must use the whole arm from hand to shoulder to grasp the team-mate's body at or below the level of the armpit. Placing only a hand on another player is not satisfactory binding.

(a) **Binding by all front-row players.** All front-row players must bind firmly and continuously from the start to the finish of the scrum. (PK)

Penalty: Penalty Kick

(b) **Binding by hookers.** The hooker may bind either over or under the arms of the props. The props must not support the hooker so that the hooker has no weight on either foot. (PK)

Penalty: Penalty Kick

LAW 20 - SCRUM

(c) **Binding by loose-head props.** A loose-head prop must either bind on the opposing tight-head prop by placing the left arm inside the right arm of the tight-head prop or by placing the left hand or forearm on the left thigh. The loose-head prop may change to the alternative position at any time. (PK)

Penalty: Penalty Kick

(d) **Binding by tight-head props.** (PK) Tight-head props must bind on the opposing loose-head props' by placing their right arm outside the left upper arm of the opposing loose-head prop. The tight-head props must grip the loose-head props' jerseys to keep themselves and the scrum steady. The tight-head props must not bind on the opposition loose-head props' arms or sleeves. They must not exert downward pressure.

Penalty: Penalty Kick

(e) **Binding by all other players.** All players in a scrum, other than front-row players, must bind on a lock's body with at least one arm. The locks must bind with the props in front of them. No player other than a prop may hold an opponent. (PK)

Penalty: Penalty Kick

(f) **Flanker obstructing opposing scrum-half.** A flanker may bind onto the scrum at any angle, provided the flanker is properly bound. The flanker must not widen that angle and so obstruct the opposing scrum-half moving forward. (PK)

Penalty: Penalty Kick

(g) **Scrum collapse.** If a scrum collapses, the referee must blow the whistle immediately so that players stop pushing.

(h) **Player forced upwards.** If a player in a scrum is lifted in the air, or is forced upwards out of the scrum, the referee must blow the whistle immediately so that players stop pushing.

LAW 20 - SCRUM

4 THE TEAM THROWING THE BALL INTO THE SCRUM

(a) After an infringement, the team that did not cause the infringement throws in the ball.

(b) **Scrum after ruck.** Refer to Law 16.7 page 71

(a) **Scrum after maul.** Refer to Law 17.6 page 74

(b) **Scrum after any other stoppage.** After any other stoppage or irregularity not covered by law, the team that was moving forward before the stoppage throws in the ball. If neither team was moving forward, the attacking team throws in the ball.

5 THROWING THE BALL INTO THE SCRUM

(a) **No Delay.** As soon as the front rows have come together, the scrum-half must throw in the ball without delay. The scrum-half must throw in the ball when told to do so by the referee. The scrum-half must throw in the ball from the side of the scrum first chosen. (FK)

(b) Voluntary delay in throwing in the ball must be penalised.

Penalty: Free Kick

6. HOW THE SCRUM-HALF THROWS IN THE BALL

(a) The scrum-half must stand one metre from the scrum, on the middle line. (FK)

(b) The scrum-half must hold the ball with both hands, over the middle line between the front rows, midway between the knee and ankle. (FK)

(c) The scrum-half must throw in the ball at a quick speed. (FK)

(d) The scrum-half must throw in the ball straight along the middle line, so that it first touches the ground immediately beyond the width of the nearer prop's shoulders. (FK)

(e) The scrum-half must throw in the ball with a single forward movement. This means that there must be no backward movement with the ball. The scrum-half must not pretend to throw the ball. (FK)

Penalty: Free Kick

LAW 20 - SCRUM

7. WHEN THE SCRUM BEGINS

(a) Play in the scrum begins when the ball leaves the hands of the scrum-half.

(b) If the scrum-half throws in the ball and it comes out at either end of the tunnel, the ball must be thrown in again unless a free kick or penalty has been awarded.

(c) If the ball is not played by a front-row player, and it goes straight through the tunnel and comes out behind the foot of a far prop without being touched, the scrum-half must throw it in again.

(d) If the ball is played by a front-row player and comes out of the tunnel, advantage may apply.

8 FRONT-ROW PLAYERS

(a) **Striking before the throw-in ('foot up').** All front-row players must place their feet to leave a clear tunnel. Until the ball has left the scrum-half's hands, they must not raise or advance a foot. They must not do anything to stop the ball being thrown in to the scrum correctly or touching the ground at the correct place.

Penalty: Free Kick

LAW 20 - SCRUM

(b) **Striking after the throw-in.** Once the ball touches the ground in the tunnel, any front-row player may use either foot to try to win possession of the ball.

(c) **Kicking-out.** A front-row player must not voluntarily kick the ball out of the tunnel in the direction from which it was thrown in. (FK)

Penalty: Free Kick

(d) If the ball is kicked out involuntarily, the same team must throw it in again.

(e) If the ball is repeatedly kicked out, the referee must treat this as voluntary and penalise the offender. (FK)

Penalty: Free Kick

(f) **Swinging.** A front-row player must not strike for the ball with both feet. No player may voluntarily raise both feet from the ground, either when the ball is being thrown in or afterwards. (PK)

Penalty: Penalty Kick

(g) **Twisting, dipping or collapsing.** Front-row players must not twist or lower their bodies, or pull opponents, or do anything that is likely to collapse the scrum, either when the ball is being thrown in or afterwards. (PK)

Penalty: Penalty Kick

(h) Referees must penalise strictly any voluntary collapsing of the scrum. This is dangerous play. (PK)

Penalty: Penalty Kick

(i) **Lifting or forcing an opponent up.** A front-row player must not lift an opponent in the air, or force an opponent upwards out of the scrum, either when the ball is being thrown in or afterwards. This is dangerous play. (PK)

Penalty: Penalty Kick

LAW 20 - SCRUM

9   SCRUM - GENERAL RESTRICTIONS

(a) **All players: Collapsing.** A player must not voluntarily collapse a scrum. A player must not voluntarily fall or kneel in a scrum. This is dangerous play.   (PK)

   Penalty: Penalty Kick

(b) **All players: Handling in the scrum.** Players must not handle the ball in the scrum or pick it up with their legs.   (PK)

   Penalty: Penalty Kick

(c) **All players: Other restrictions on winning the ball.** Players must not try to win the ball in the scrum by using any part of their body except their foot or lower leg.   (FK)

   Penalty: Free Kick

(d) **All players: When the ball comes out, leave it out.** When the ball has left the scrum, a player must not bring it back in to the scrum.   (FK)

   Penalty: Free Kick

(e) **All players: No falling on the ball.** A player must not fall on or over the ball as it is coming out of the scrum.   (PK)

   Penalty: Penalty Kick

(f) **Locks and flankers: Staying out of the tunnel.** A player who is not a front-row player must not play the ball in the tunnel.   (FK)

   Penalty: Free Kick

(g) **Scrum-half: Kicking in the scrum.** A scrum-half must not kick the ball while it is in the scrum.   (PK)

   Penalty: Penalty Kick

(h) **Scrum-half: Dummying.** A scrum-half must not take any action to make the opponents think that the ball is out of the scrum while it is still in the scrum.   (FK)

   Penalty: Free Kick

LAW 20 - SCRUM

(i) **Scrum-half: Holding opposing flanker.** A scrum-half must not grasp an opposing flanker in order to gain leverage, or for any other reason. (PK)

Penalty: Penalty Kick

10 ENDING THE SCRUM

(a) **The ball comes out.** When the ball comes out of the scrum in any direction except the tunnel, the scrum ends.

(b) **Scrum in an in-goal.** A scrum cannot take place in an In-goal. When the ball in a scrum is on or over the goal-line, the scrum ends and an attacker or a defender may legally ground the ball for a try or a touch-down.

(c) **Hindmost player unbinds.** The hindmost player in a scrum is the player whose feet are nearest the team's own goal-line. If the hindmost player unbinds from the scrum with the ball at that player's feet and picks up the ball, the scrum ends.

HINDMOST PLAYER UNBINDS

11 SCRUM WHEELED

(a) If a scrum is wheeled through more than 90 degrees, so that the middle line has passed beyond a position parallel to the touch-line, the referee must stop play and order another scrum.

(b) This new scrum is formed at the place where the previous scrum ended. The ball is thrown in by the team that had won possession. If neither team won possession, it is thrown in by the team that previously threw it in.

LAW 20 - SCRUM

12 OFF-SIDE AT THE SCRUM

DEFINITION

At a scrum, the off-side line for the scrum-halves runs through the line of the ball in the scrum. For every other player the off-side line runs through the hindmost foot of that player's team in the scrum. If the hindmost foot of a team is on or behind that team's goal-line, the off-side line is the goal-line. The off-side lines are parallel to the goal-lines.

The purpose of the scrum off-side law is to ensure that, until the scrum ends, the team winning the ball has a clear space in which to make use of it.

(a) **Off-side for scrum-halves.** When a team has won the ball in a scrum, the scrum-half of that team is off-side if both feet are in front of the ball while it is still in the scrum. If the scrum-half has only one foot in front of the ball, the scrum-half is not off-side. (PK)

(b) When a team has won the ball in a scrum, the scrum-half of the opposing team is off-side if that scrum-half steps in front of the ball with either foot while the ball is still in the scrum. (PK)

(c) The scrum-half whose team does not win possession of the ball must not move to the opposite side of the scrum and overstep the off-side line running through the hindmost foot of that player's team in the scrum. (PK)

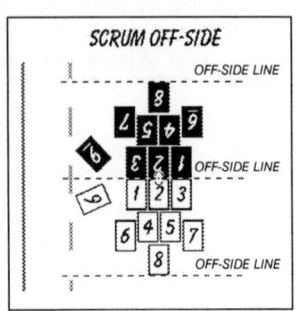

SCRUM OFF-SIDE

OFF-SIDE LINE

OFF-SIDE LINE

OFF-SIDE LINE

(d) The scrum-half whose team does not win possession of the ball must not move away from the scrum and then remain in front of the off-side line running through the hindmost foot of that player's team in the scrum. (PK)

(e) Any player may be scrum-half, but a team can have only one scrum-half at each scrum. (PK)

Penalty: Penalty Kick on the off-side line.

LAW 21 - PENALTY AND FREE KICKS

(f) **Off-side for players not in the scrum.** Players who are not in the scrum, and who are not the team's scrum-half, are off-side if they remain in front of their off-side line or overstep the off-side line. (PK)

Penalty: Penalty Kick on the off-side line

(g) **Loitering.** When a scrum is forming, players not taking part in it must retire to their off-side line without delay. If they do not, they are loitering. Loiterers must be penalised. (PK)

Penalty: Penalty Kick on the off-side line.

LAW 21 - PENALTY AND FREE KICKS

DEFINITION

Penalty kicks and free kicks are awarded to the non-offending team for infringements by their opponents.

1 WHERE PENALTY AND FREE KICKS ARE AWARDED

Unless a law states otherwise, the mark for a penalty or free kick is at the place of infringement.

2 WHERE PENALTY AND FREE KICKS ARE TAKEN

(a) The kicker must take the penalty or free kick at the mark or anywhere behind it on a line through the mark. If the place for a penalty or free kick is within 5 metres of the opponents' goal-line, the mark for the kick is 5 metres from the goal-line, opposite the place of infringement.

(b) When a penalty or free kick is awarded for an infringement in in-goal, the mark for the kick is in the field-of play, 5 metres from the goal-line, in line with the place of infringement.

Penalty: Any infringement by the kicker's team results in a scrum at the mark. The opposing team throws in the ball.

3 HOW THE PENALTY AND FREE KICKS ARE TAKEN

(a) Any player may take a penalty or free kick awarded for an infringement with any kind of kick: punt, drop kick or place kick. The ball may be kicked with any part of the leg from knee to toe but not with the heel.

(b) Bouncing the ball on the knee is not taking a kick.

(c) The kicker must use the ball that was in play unless the referee decides it was defective.

Penalty: Any infringement by the kicker's team results in a scrum at the mark. The opposing team throws in the ball.

LAW 21 - PENALTY AND FREE KICKS

4 PENALTY AND FREE KICK OPTIONS AND REQUIREMENTS

(a) **Scrum alternative.** A team awarded a penalty or free kick may choose a scrum instead. They throw in the ball.

(b) **No delay.** If a kicker indicates to the referee the intention to kick a penalty kick at goal, the kick must be taken within one minute from the time the player indicates the intention to kick at goal. If the one minute is exceeded the kick is disallowed, a scrum ordered at the place of the mark and the opponents throw in the ball.

(c) **A clear kick.** The kicker must kick the ball a visible distance. If the kicker is holding it, it must clearly leave the hands. If it is on the ground, it must clearly leave the mark.

(d) **Place kicking for touch.** The kicker may punt or drop kick for touch but must not place kick for touch.

(e) **Kicker's freedom of action.** The kicker is free to kick the ball in any direction and may play the ball again.

(f) **Kick taken in the in-goal.** When a penalty or free kick is taken in the team's in-goal and a defending player by foul play prevents an opponent from scoring a try, a penalty try is awarded.

(g) **Out of play in the in-goal.** If the penalty or free kick is taken in the In-goal, and the ball goes into touch-in-goal or on or over the dead-ball line, a 5-metre scrum is awarded. The attacking team throws in the ball.

(h) **Behind the ball.** All the kicker's team at a penalty or free kick must be behind the ball until it has been kicked, except the placer for a place kick.

(i) **Kick taken quickly.** If the penalty or free kick is taken so quickly that players of the kicker's team are still in front of the ball, they are not penalised for being off-side. However, they must retire immediately. They must not stop retiring until they are on-side. They must not take part in the game until they are on-side. This applies to all players of that team, whether they are inside or outside the playing area.

PENALTY KICK TAKEN QUICKLY

LAW 21 - PENALTY AND FREE KICKS

(j) In this situation, players become on-side when they run behind the team-mate who took the penalty or free kick, or when a team-mate carrying the ball runs in front of them, or when a team-mate who was behind the ball when it was kicked runs in front of them.

(k) An off-side player cannot be put on-side by any action of an opponent.

Penalty: Unless otherwise stated in law any infringement by the kicker's team results in a scrum at the mark. The opposing team throw in the ball.

5   SCORING A GOAL FROM A PENALTY KICK

(a) A penalty goal can be scored from a penalty kick.

(b) If the kicker indicates to the referee the intention to kick at goal, the kicker must kick at goal. Once the kicker has made the intention clear, here can be no change of the intention. The referee may enquire of the kicker as to the intention.

(c) If the kicker indicates to the referee the intent to kick at goal, the opposing team must stand still with their hands by their sides from the time the kicker starts to approach to kick until the ball is kicked.

(d) If the kicker has not indicated an intention to kick at goal but takes a drop kick and scores a goal, the goal stands.

(e) If the opposing team infringes while the kick is being taken but the kick at goal is successful, the goal stands. A further penalty is not awarded for the infringement.

(f) The kicker may place the ball on sand, sawdust or a kicking tee approved by the Union.

LAW 21 - PENALTY AND FREE KICKS

6 SCORING FROM A FREE KICK

(a) A goal cannot be scored from a free kick.

(b) The team awarded a free kick cannot score a dropped goal until after the ball next becomes dead, or after an opponent has played or touched it, or has tackled the ball-carrier. This restriction applies also to a scrum taken instead of a free kick.

7 WHAT THE OPPOSING TEAM MUST DO AT A PENALTY KICK

(a) **Must run from the mark.** The opposing team must immediately run towards their own goal-line until they are at least 10 metres away from the mark for the penalty kick, or until they have reached their goal-line if that is nearer the mark.

(b) **Must keep running.** Even if the penalty kick is taken and the kicker's team is playing the ball, opposing players must keep running until they have retired the necessary distance. They must not take part in the game until they have done so.

(c) **Kick taken quickly.** If the penalty kick is taken so quickly that opponents have no opportunity to retire, they will not be penalised for this. However, they must continue to retire as described in (b) above or until a team-mate who was 10 metres from the mark has run in front of them, before they take part in the game.

(d) **Interference.** The opposing team must not do anything to delay the penalty kick or obstruct the kicker. They must not voluntarily take, throw or kick the ball out of reach of the kicker or the kicker's team-mates.

Penalty: Any infringement by the opposing team results in a second penalty kick, 10 metres in front of the mark for the first kick. This mark must not be within 5 metres of the goal-line. Any player may take the kick. The kicker may change the type of kick and may choose to kick at goal. If the referee awards a second penalty kick, the second penalty kick is not taken before the referee has made the mark indicating the place of the penalty.

8 WHAT OPTIONS THE OPPOSING TEAM HAVE AT A FREE KICK

(a) **Must run from the mark.** The opposing team must immediately run towards their own goal-line until they are at least 10 metres away from the mark for the free kick, or until they have reached their goal-line if that is nearer the mark. If the free kick is in a defending teams in-goal area, the opposing team must immediately run towards their own goal-line until they are at least 10 metres away from the mark and not nearer than 5 metres from the goal-line.

LAW 21 - PENALTY AND FREE KICKS

(b) **Must keep running.** Even if the free kick is taken and the kicker's team is playing the ball, opposing players must keep running until they have retired the necessary distance. They must not take part in the game until they have done so.

(c) **Kick taken quickly.** If the free kick is taken so quickly that opponents have no opportunity to retire, they will not be penalised for this. However, they must continue to retire as described in (b) above or until a team-mate who was 10 metres from the mark has run in front of them, before they take part in the game.

(d) **Interference.** The opposing team must not do anything to delay the free kick or obstruct the kicker. They must not voluntarily take, throw or kick the ball out of reach of the kicker or the kicker's team-mates.

(e) **Charging the free kick.** Once they have retired the necessary distance, players of the opposing team may charge and try to prevent the kick being taken. They may charge the free kick as soon as the kicker starts to approach to kick.

(f) **Preventing the free kick.** If the opposing team charge and prevent the free kick being taken, the kick is disallowed. Play restarts with a scrum at the mark. The opposing team throw in the ball.

(g) **Free kick taken in the in-goal.** If a free kick has been awarded in the in-goal or if it has been awarded in the field-of-play and the player retires to in-goal to take it, and the opponents charge and prevent the kick from being taken, a 5-metre scrum is ordered. The attacking team throw in the ball. If a free kick is taken in the in-goal, an opponent who legitimately plays it there can score a try.

(h) **Charged down.** If opponents charge down a free kick in the playing area, play continues.

Penalty: Any infringement by the opposing team results in a second free kick, awarded 10 metres in front of the mark for the first kick. This mark must not be within 5 metres of the goal-line. Any player may take the kick. If the referee awards a second free kick, the second free kick is not taken before the referee has made the mark indicating the place of the free kick.

9 CONTRIVED INFRINGEMENTS AT THE PENALTY KICK

If the referee believes that the kicker's team has contrived an infringement by their opponents, the referee does not award a further penalty but allows play continue.

LAW 21 - PENALTY AND FREE KICKS

10   CONTRIVED INFRINGEMENTS AT THE FREE KICK

(a) The kicker must not pretend to kick. As soon as the kicker makes a move to kick, the opponents may charge.

(b) If the referee believes that the kicker's team has contrived an infringement by their opponents, the referee does not award a further free kick but allows play continue.

DURING THE MATCH

In-Goal

Law 22   In-Goal

LAW 22 - IN-GOAL

IN-GOAL

The game is now being played according to the previous laws with teams attempting to maximise their scoring opportunities by attacking their opponents' in-goal, whilst the opposing team will attempt to defend their own in-goal. There is one law that covers all the activities that can take place in an in-goal. (Law 22).

LAW 22 - IN-GOAL

DEFINITIONS

In-goal is part of the ground as defined in Law 1 where the ball may be grounded by players from either team.

When attacking players are first to ground the ball in the opponents' in-goal, the attacking players score a try.

When defending players are first to ground the ball in in-goal, the defending players make a touch down.

A defending player who has one foot on the goal l ine or in the in-goal who receives the ball is considered to be in in-goal.

1 GROUNDING THE BALL

There are two ways a player can ground the ball:

(a) **Player touches the ground with the ball.** A player grounds the ball by holding the ball and touching the ground with it, in in-goal. 'Holding' means holding in the hand or hands, or in the arm or arms. No downward pressure is required.

(b) **Player presses down on the ball.** A player grounds the ball when it is on the ground in the in-goal and the player presses down on it with a hand or hands, arm or arms, or the front of the player's body from waist to neck inclusive.

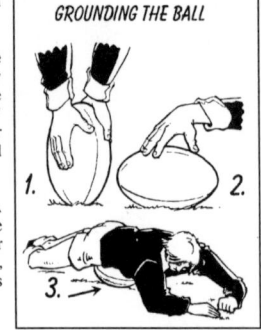

2 PICKING UP THE BALL

Picking up the ball from the ground is not grounding it. A player may pick up the ball in the in-goal and ground it elsewhere in the in-goal.

LAW 22 - IN-GOAL

3 BALL GROUNDED BY AN ATTACKING PLAYER

Try. When an attacking player who is on-side is first to ground the ball in the opponents' in-goal, the player scores a try. This applies whether an attacking or a defending player is responsible for the ball being in the in-goal.

4 OTHER WAYS TO SCORE A TRY

(a) **Grounded on the goal-line.** The goal-line is part of the in-goal. If an attacking player is first to ground the ball on the opponents' goal-line, a try is scored.

(b) **Grounded against a goal post.** The goal posts and padding surrounding them are part of the goal line which is part of in-goal. If an attacking player is first to ground the ball against the goal post or padding, a try is scored.

(c) **Pushover try.** A scrum or ruck cannot take place in the in-goal. If a scrum or ruck is pushed into the in-goal, an attacking player may legally ground the ball as soon as the ball reaches or crosses the goal-line and a try is scored.

(d) **Momentum try.** If an attacking player with the ball is tackled short of the goal-line but the player's momentum carries the player into the opponent's in-goal, and the player is first to ground the ball, a try is scored.

(e) **Tackled near the goal-line.** If a player is tackled near to the opponents' goal-line so that this player can immediately reach out and ground the ball on or over the goal-line, a try is scored.

(f) This player must not infringe the tackle law. The tackle law requires a tackled player to play the ball immediately. However, the tackled player may place the ball on the ground in any direction provided it is done immediately.

(g) In this situation, defending players who are on their feet may legally prevent the try by pulling the ball from the tackled player's hands or arms, but must not kick the ball.

LAW 22 - IN-GOAL

(h) **Player in touch or touch-in-goal.** If an attacking player is in touch or in touch-in-goal, the player can score a try by grounding the ball in the opponents' in-goal provided the player is not carrying the ball.

CASES WHERE A TRY IS SCORED

(i) **Penalty try.** A penalty try is awarded if a try would probably have been scored but for foul play by the defending team. A penalty try is awarded if a try would probably have been scored in a better position but for foul play by the defending team.

(j) A penalty try is awarded between the goal posts. The defending team may charge the conversion kick after a penalty try.

5 BALL GROUNDED BY A DEFENDING PLAYER

(a) **Touch down.** When defending players are first to ground the ball in their in-goal, it results in a touch down.

(b) **Player in touch or touch-in-goal.** If defending players are in touch-in-goal, they can make a touch down by grounding the ball in their in-goal provided they are not carrying the ball.

6 SCRUM OR RUCK IS PUSHED INTO IN-GOAL

A scrum or ruck can take place only in the field-of-play. Therefore, if a scrum or ruck is pushed across the goal-line, a defending player may legally ground the ball as soon as the ball reaches or crosses the goal-line. This results in a touch down.

7 RESTARTING AFTER A TOUCH DOWN

(a) When an attacking player sends or carries the ball into the opponents' in-goal and it becomes dead there, either because a defender grounded it or because it went into touch-in-goal or on or over the dead-ball line, a drop-out is awarded.

(b) If an attacking player knocks-on or throws-forward in the field-of-play and the ball goes into the opponents' In-goal and it is made dead there, a scrum is awarded where the knock-on or throw-forward happened.

116

LAW 22 - IN-GOAL

(c) If at a kick-off the ball is kicked into the opponents' in-goal without having touched or been touched by a player and a defending player grounds it there or makes it dead without delay, the defending team have two choices:

To have a scrum formed at the centre, and they throw in the ball; or
To have the other team kick-off again.

(d) If a defending player threw or took the ball into the In-goal, and a defending player grounded it, and there has been no infringement, play is restarted by a 5-metre scrum. The position of the scrum is in line with where the ball has been touched down. The attacking side throws in the ball.

8 BALL KICKED DEAD IN IN-GOAL

If a team kicks the ball through their opponents' in-goal, into touch-in-goal or on or over the dead ball line, except by an unsuccessful kick at goal or attempted dropped goal, the defending team has two choices:

To have a drop-out, or
To have a scrum at the place where the ball was kicked and they throw in.

9 DEFENDING PLAYER IN-GOAL

A defending player who has part of one foot in in-goal is considered to have both feet in in-goal.

10 BALL HELD UP IN-GOAL

When a player carrying the ball is held up in the in-goal so that the player cannot ground the ball, the ball is dead. A 5-metre scrum is formed. This would apply if play similar to a maul takes place in goal. The attacking team throws in the ball.

11 BALL DEAD IN IN-GOAL

(a) When the ball or a player carrying it touches the corner post, the touch-in-goal line or the dead-ball line, or touches the ground beyond those lines, the ball becomes dead. If the ball was carried or played into in-goal by the attacking team, a drop-out shall be awarded to the defending team. If the ball was carried or played into in-goal by the defending team, a 5-metre scrum shall be awarded and the attacking team throws in the ball.

(b) When a player scores a try or makes a touch-down, the ball becomes dead.

LAW 22 - IN-GOAL

12 ATTACKING INFRINGEMENT WITH SCRUM PENALTY

If an attacking player commits an infringement in in-goal, for which the penalty is a scrum, for example, a knock-on, play is restarted with a 5-metre scrum. The scrum is formed in line with the place of the infringement and the defending team throws in the ball.

13 DEFENDING INFRINGEMENT WITH SCRUM PENALTY

If a defending player infringes in in-goal, for which the penalty is a scrum, for example, a knock-on, play is restarted with a 5-metre scrum. The scrum is formed in line with the place of the infringement and the attacking team throws in the ball.

14 DOUBT ABOUT GROUNDING

If there is doubt about which team first grounded the ball in the in-goal, play is re-started by a 5-metre scrum, in line with the place where the ball was grounded. The attacking team throws in the ball.

15 INFRINGEMENTS IN IN-GOAL

All infringements in the in-goal are treated as if they had taken place in the field-of-play.

A knock-on or a throw-forward in the in-goal results in a 5-metre scrum, opposite the place of infringement.

Penalty: For an infringement, the mark for a penalty kick or free kick cannot be in the in-goal.

When a penalty kick or free kick is awarded for an infringement in the In-goal, the mark for the kick is in the field-of-play, 5 metres from the goal-line, opposite the place of infringement.

16 MISCONDUCT OR UNFAIR PLAY IN IN-GOAL

(a) **Obstruction by the attacking team.** When a player charges or voluntarily obstructs an opponent in the in-goal who has just kicked the ball, the opponent's team may choose to take the penalty kick either in the field-of-play, 5 metres from the goal-line opposite the place of infringement, or where the ball landed.

LAW 22 - IN-GOAL

If they make the second choice and the ball lands in or near touch, the mark for the penalty kick is 15 metres from the touch-line, opposite where the ball went into touch or where it landed.

A try is disallowed and a penalty kick awarded if a try would probably not have been scored but for foul play by the attacking team.

(b) **Foul play by the defending team.** The referee awards a penalty try if a try would probably have been scored but for foul play by the defending team.

The referee awards a penalty try if a try would probably have been scored in a better position but for foul play by the defending team.

A penalty try is awarded between the goal posts. The defending team may charge the conversion kick after a penalty try.

(c) **Any other foul play.** When a player commits any other foul play in the in-goal while the ball is out of play, the penalty kick is awarded at (PK) the place where the game would otherwise have re-started.

Penalty: Penalty Kick.

iRB
INTERNATIONAL RUGBY BOARD

RUGBY

LAWS OF THE GAME MADE EASIER

UNDER 19 VARIATIONS

UNDER 19 VARIATIONS

LAW 3 - NUMBER OF PLAYERS - THE TEAM

(5) (d) If a team nominates 22 players, it **must** have at least six players who can play in the front row in order that there is replacement cover for the loose-head prop, hooker and tight-head prop.

(5) (e) If a team nominates more than 22 players it **must** have at least six players who can play in the front row in order that there is replacement cover for the loose-head prop, hooker and tight-head prop. There must also be three players who can play in lock position.

(13) (b) A player who has been substituted may replace an injured player.

LAW 5 - TIME

Each half of an Under-19 match lasts 35 minutes playing time. Play in a match last no longer than 70 minutes. After a total of 70 minutes playing time, the referee **must not** allow extra time to be played in the case of a drawn match in a knock-out competition.

LAW 20 - SCRUM

(1) (b) A scrum must not be formed less than 5 metres from a touch line or a goal line. When an infringement or stoppage is less than 5 metres from a touch line or a goal line, the scrum is formed 5 metres from that line.

(1) (f) In an 8 person scrum the formation must be 3-4-1, with the single player (normally the Number 8) shoving on the 2 locks. The locks must pack with their heads on either side of the hooker.

Exception A team may have fewer than eight players in its scrum when **either** the team cannot field a complete team, **or** a player is sent off for Foul Play, or a player leaves the field because of injury.

Even allowing for this exception, each team must always have at least five players in a scrum.

If a team is incomplete, the scrum formation must be as follows:

> If a team is without one player, then both teams must use a 3-4 formation (i.e. no No.8).
> If a team is without two players, then both teams must use a 3-2-1 formation (i.e. no flankers).
> If a team is without three players, then both teams must use a 3-2 formation (i.e. only front rows and locks).

When a normal scrum takes place, the players in the three front-row positions and the two lock positions must have been suitably trained for these positions.

If a team cannot field such suitably trained players because:
> either they are not available, **or**
> a player in one of those five positions is injured **or** has been sent off for Foul Play and no suitably trained replacement is available, then the referee must order uncontested scrums.

In an uncontested scrum, the teams do not compete for the ball. The team putting in the ball must win it. Neither team is allowed to push the other team away from the mark.

Front rows coming together Each prop touches the opponent's upper arm and then pause before the front rows meet. The sequence should be: crouch, touch, pause, engage.

No wheeling. A team must not intentionally wheel a scrum. (PK)

Penalty: Penalty Kick

If a wheel reaches 45 degrees, the referee must stop play. If the wheel is unintentional, the referee orders another scrum at the place where the scrum is stopped.

Maximum 1.5 metres push A team in a scrum must not push the scrum more than 1.5 metres towards their opponents' goal line. (FK)

Penalty: Free Kick

Ball must be released from scrum A player must not intentionally keep the ball in the scrum once the player's team has heeled the ball and controls it at the base of the scrum. (FK)

Penalty: Free Kick.

iRB
INTERNATIONAL RUGBY BOARD

RUGBY

LAWS OF THE GAME MADE EASIER

STANDARD SET OF VARIATIONS APPROPRIATE TO THE SEVEN-A-SIDE GAME

VARIATIONS APPROPRIATE TO THE SEVEN-A-SIDE GAME

The Laws of the Game apply to the Seven-a-side game, subject to the following variations:

LAW 3 - NUMBER OF PLAYERS - THE TEAM

1 MAXIMUM NUMBER OF PLAYERS ON THE PLAYING AREA

Maximum: each team must have no more than seven players on the playing area.

4 PLAYERS NOMINATED AS SUBSTITUTES

A team may nominate no more than three replacements/substitutes.

5 NUMBER OF SUBSTITUTIONS

A team can substitute or replace up to three players.

13 SUBSTITUTED PLAYERS REJOINING THE MATCH

If a player is substituted, that player must not return and play in that match even to replace an injured player.

Exception: a substituted player may replace a player with a bleeding or open wound.

LAW 5 - TOSS TIME

1 DURATION OF A MATCH

A match lasts no longer than 14 minutes plus lost time and extra time. A match is divided into two halves of not more than seven minutes playing time.

Exception: A competition final match may last no longer than 20 minutes plus lost time and extra time. The match is divided into two halves of not more than 10 minutes playing time.

VARIATIONS APPROPRIATE TO THE SEVEN-A-SIDE GAME

2 HALF TIME

After half time the teams change ends. There is an interval of not more than one minute. During a competition final there is an interval of not more than two minutes.

6 EXTRA TIME - DURATION

When there is a drawn match and extra time is required, the extra time is played in periods of 5 minutes. After each period, the teams change ends without an interval.

LAW 6 - MATCH OFFICIALS

A. REFEREE

3 DUTIES OF THE REFEREE BEFORE THE MATCH

Add extra paragraph:

(b) **Extra Time - Toss.**

Before extra time starts, the referee organises a toss. One of the Captains tosses a coin and the other Captain calls to see who wins the toss. The winner of the toss decides whether to kick-off or choose an end. If the winner of the toss decides to choose an end, the opponents must kick off and vice versa.

B. TOUCH JUDGES

AFTER THE MATCH

8 IN-GOAL JUDGES

(a) There are two in-goal judges for each match.

(b) The referee has the same control over both in-goal judges as the referee has over touch judges.

(c) There is only one in-goal judge in each in-goal area.

VARIATIONS APPROPRIATE TO THE SEVEN-A-SIDE GAME

(d) **Signalling result of kick at goal.** When a conversion kick or a penalty kick at goal is being taken, an in-goal touch judge must help the referee by signalling the result of the kick. One touch judge stands at or behind a goal post and an in-goal judge stands at or behind the other goal post. If the ball goes over the cross-bar and between the posts, the touch judge and the in-goal judge raise their flags to indicate a goal.

(e) **Signalling touch.** When the ball or the ball-carrier has gone into touch-in-goal, the in-goal judge must hold up the flag.

(f) **Signalling tries.** The in-goal judge will assist the referee in decisions on touch downs and tries if there is any doubt in the referees mind.

(g) **Signalling foul play.** A match organiser may give authority for the in-goal judge to signal foul play in the in-goal.

LAW 9 - METHOD OF SCORING

B   CONVERSION KICK

1   TAKING A CONVERSION KICK

Amend
(c) If the scoring team elects to kick at goal after a try, the kick must be a drop kick.

Delete (d)

3   THE OPPOSING TEAM

Amend
(a) All the opposing team must immediately assemble close to their own 10-metre line.

Delete (b)

(c) Delete 3rd paragraph "When another kick is allowed.."